W9-AAD-428

10

10

RICHARD "PANCHO" GONZALEZ

Tennis Champion

NOV 5   1998

Doreen Gonzales

Enslow Publishers, Inc.
44 Fadem Road   PO Box 38
Box 699   Aldershot
Springfield, NJ 07081 Hants GU12 6BP
USA   UK

For Chris.

Library of Congress Cataloging-in-Publication Data

Gonzales, Doreen
    Richard "Pancho" Gonzalez, tennis champion / Doreen Gonzales.
      p. cm. — (Hispanic biographies)
    Includes bibliographical references (p. 120) and index
    Summary: Details the life and career of the Mexican American who
became a brilliant success as a tennis champion, examining his
dedication as a player and a competitor.
    ISBN 0-89490-891-X
    1. Gonzales, Pancho, 1928–   —Juvenile literature. 2. Tennis
players—United States—Biography—Juvenile literature. 3. Mexican
American tennis players—Biography—Juvenile literature. [1. Gonzales,
Pancho, 1928–   . 2. Tennis players. 3. Mexican American tennis
players. 4. Mexican Americans—Biography.] I. Title. II. Series.
GV994.G65G66   1998
796.342'092—dc21
[B]   97-45093
                                                                     CIP
                                                                     AC

Printed in the United States of America

10 9 8 7 6 5 4 3 2 1

Illustration Credits: © Corel Corporation, p. 66; Courtesy of Ralph
Gonzales, pp. 12, 58, 61; Courtesy of The International Tennis Hall of
Fame & Museum, Newport, R.I., pp. 4, 19, 35, 39, 48, 73, 82, 89,
92, 100, 103, 109; Spalding Sports Worldwide, p. 63; Courtesy of
Fort Collins Museum, p. 75; ProServe, p. 84.

Cover Illustration: Courtesy of The International Tennis Hall of Fame
& Museum, Newport, R.I.

CONTENTS

1 The Best Player Ever 5

2 He Could Overcome Anything 14

3 Climbing 29

4 United States Champion 44

5 Past Tense 54

6 "Fifty Points on Terror" 68

7 Transitions 79

8 The Name of the Game
    Is Strategy 91

9 The Old Wolf 105

10 Tennis's Best 114

Chronology 117

Chapter Notes 120

Further Reading 126

Index 127

Richard "Pancho" Gonzalez was a champion tennis player and would receive many trophies during his long career.

THE BEST PLAYER EVER

 Richard Gonzalez faced his opponent, ready to fight for the most important thing in his life—the United States Amateur Tennis Championship. It was September 5, 1949. Thirteen thousand spectators had gathered in Forest Hills, New York, to witness his battle for the national title.

Gonzalez was not thinking about them, though. His mind was focused on the man on the other side of the net, Ted Schroeder. The match began and both men fought intensely for every point. They seemed evenly matched, and the lead kept changing hands. Finally, one hour thirteen minutes after beginning play, Schroeder beat Gonzalez in the first set, 18–16.

During a rest period between sets, Schroeder put on spiked shoes for better traction. Gonzalez did not own spikes. This seemed to give Schroeder an advantage because he quickly won the second set, 6–2.[1]

Afterward, Gonzalez's friend Frank Shields took Gonzalez aside. Shields told Gonzalez to move closer to the net when Schroeder was ahead and serving. Shields had noticed that Schroeder served less powerfully in this situation, and Gonzalez was playing too far back on the court to make a good return. Gonzalez used Shields's advice and won both the third and fourth sets.

Now the score was tied at two sets apiece. The winner of the next set would win the national championship. Even though Schroeder served, Gonzalez won the first game. This is called breaking serve. Breaking serve is such a difficult feat it can destroy an opponent's self-confidence. Indeed, Schroeder weakened as Gonzalez continued a relentless attack. By the end of the ninth game, Gonzalez was leading, 5–4.

Gonzalez opened the next game with a searing serve that flew past Schroeder untouched. Then several points seesawed back and forth until Gonzalez smashed a ball past Schroeder to go up by one. If he could capture the following point, he would be the national tennis champion.

Gonzalez served. Schroeder hit the ball back. Gonzalez returned it. Schroeder drove the ball down Gonzalez's sideline, and Gonzalez watched it go by. Everyone looked to the lineman for the deciding call. He signaled out-of-bounds, making Richard Gonzalez the 1949 United States tennis champion.

Gonzalez savored the title. Many people believed that his rise to the top had been due to luck, and they considered him an outsider in the world of championship tennis. This world had always been populated by people who were financially well-off. Prior champions had received private lessons and guidance long before becoming teenagers. They were polite, sophisticated, and exhibited social grace. And they were white.

Then came Richard Gonzalez, a man who seemed different from past champions in every way. He had been born in a small Los Angeles apartment. His parents were immigrants from Mexico, and they both worked to support their family. When Gonzalez started playing tennis at twelve, his parents could not afford lessons. So he learned the game by watching others.

Even if Gonzalez's family had been rich, though, Gonzalez would not have been allowed to join the tennis clubs in his hometown. His skin was too dark. Discrimination against Mexican Americans, African Americans, and other people with dark skin was common all over the United States during Gonzalez's childhood. Los Angeles was no exception.

At times, discrimination was as much an opponent to Gonzalez as the player on the other side of the net. People frequently made derogatory remarks to him because of his Mexican heritage. Some held unsubstantiated beliefs about his character based on negative stereotypes. Gonzalez was even banned from certain places because of his ethnicity.

Each racist incident hurt Gonzalez and made him bitter. Yet he rarely spoke out about prejudice. Instead, he channeled his hurt and frustration into tennis.[2] He was a merciless opponent on the court, and this attitude helped make him a top competitor.

By the age of fourteen, Richard Gonzalez was already making his mark on southern California tennis. At nineteen he won the United States National Championship. He captured the title again the next year. Then he became an unbeatable foe in professional tennis.

Gonzalez's success required incredible athletic skills. But it also required the ability to rise above discrimination. Gonzalez did not achieve this through speeches or demonstrations or acts of rebellion. He achieved it by becoming the best at his chosen profession while always remaining proud of and loyal to his roots.

Gonzalez's father, Manuel Antonio Gonzales, had been born in Mexico. Manuel's mother died when he was only eight years old. Soon after, Manuel and his father left Mexico and walked across the desert to an aunt's house in Globe, Arizona. They traveled in their bare feet. One morning Manuel woke up at his aunt's house and his father was gone.

Manuel stayed with his aunt. He tended her farm through the scorching summers and carried firewood for miles during the cold winters. Yet Manuel always felt like he was not wanted at his aunt's. So as soon as he was old enough, he left, too. In 1918 Manuel moved to Los Angeles, California.[3]

Manuel Gonzales was one of a half million Mexicans who immigrated to the United States from Mexico between 1900 and 1920. Most came to escape poverty or the revolutionary war that raged in the country. The majority of the immigrants settled in the Southwest and worked in factories and mines or on railroads, farms, or ranches.

In order for a person to live in the United States, various written documents were required. But because most of the immigrants could not read or write English, officials often recorded needed information for them. These officials usually decided how to spell the immigrant's name, and they frequently changed a Spanish spelling to a more familiar-looking English spelling. This, in fact, happened to Manuel Gonzales. In Mexico, his name was spelled with a z at the end—Gonzalez. In the United States, though, the spelling became Gonzales.

Manuel Gonzales used the new spelling his entire life and passed it down to each of his children. Richard, therefore, grew up spelling his last name Gonzales. But around 1970, Richard returned to the Spanish version of his name as an expression of pride in his heritage.[4] Consequently, Gonzalez's name is spelled differently in various books and articles, depending upon when they were written. In general, those written before 1970 use Gonzales, and those afterward use Gonzalez.

Richard Gonzalez's mother, Carmen, was also a Mexican immigrant. But Carmen had been born into a wealthy family. Her parents had owned many acres of land in Mexico. Carmen's family came to Los Angeles when she was fourteen years old to escape the Mexican Revolution. Her parents gave their land deeds to a cousin for safekeeping and told him they would return to Mexico as soon as the war ended. But while they were away, the entrusted cousin betrayed them. He put their land into his own name and refused to give it back. With no property to go home to in Mexico, Carmen's family stayed in the United States.[5]

Carmen met Manuel Gonzales when she was eighteen years old. She was a strikingly beautiful young woman with jet-black hair and dark brown eyes. She stood five feet seven inches tall. She and Manuel soon fell in love and were married. Their first child, Richard Alonzo, was born on May 9, 1928. In 1929 Carmen gave birth to twins, Manuel and Margaret. In later years, Ophelia, Bertha, Ralph, and Yolanda were born.

The Gonzales family was not poor, but poverty was never far away. They lived in a succession of small homes in central Los Angeles, each one on the out-skirts of a poor neighborhood. After a while, poverty-stricken neighborhoods crept closer and closer to them. Then Mr. and Mrs. Gonzales would move, determined to keep their children away from the crime that came with the poverty. Unfortunately, they could never move far. They would settle into another modest home on the edge of another poor neighborhood. Again, the poverty-stricken neighborhoods closed in around them, and again, they moved. This pattern was repeated so many times in Richard's childhood that he later reported, "It was like a game of tag, and often we became tired of running."[6]

No matter where they lived, though, the Gonzales home was neat and well maintained. There was always food on the table, usually a simple meal of beans and tortillas. The children's clothes were simple, too. There were few luxuries in the Gonzales home, and both of Richard's parents worked just to provide the basics for their seven children.

Mr. Gonzales was a furniture finisher who also painted scenery for Hollywood movies. After laboring all day, he came home to garden or to make repairs around the house. Richard later remembered his

In time Richard Gonzalez would become known as a great tennis player with an unbeatable serve.

father's commitment to perfection, saying that Mr. Gonzales might tear something apart and put it back together fifteen times before he was satisfied that it was right.

Mrs. Gonzales worked as a seamstress. She often had cuts on her fingers from the needles on the sewing machines she used. When she was not at work she cooked, cleaned, and cared for her children. Yet Richard's overriding memory of his mother was of her dignity. She dressed with care and moved with a regal bearing. When she walked into a room she was treated with respect.

When Richard was four years old, his father taught him how to make a kite. Richard spent the next few years creating kites that he flew in various competitions at nearby parks. He won most.

The Gonzales family spoke Spanish at home. Richard did not learn English until he started kindergarten. As his siblings entered school, English gradually replaced Spanish in the Gonzales house. Mr. and Mrs. Gonzales encouraged their children to learn the new language, for they felt it would help them succeed in the United States. But they continued to speak Spanish to their sons and daughters so that the children knew about and would be proud of their heritage.[7]

Once, Mrs. Gonzales took Richard to a park to watch tennis, a game she remembered seeing wealthy people play in Mexico. The outing reminded her of her own childhood when her family had been well-off. These memories filled Mrs. Gonzales with joy. She was especially lighthearted and fun that day. Six-year-old Richard noticed her mood, but mistakenly believed it was due to her love of tennis. Hoping to make his mother's happiness last forever, he told her, "Mama, someday I will be the best [tennis] player ever and you will be real happy."[8]

HE COULD
OVERCOME
ANYTHING

Prisoner was Richard's favorite game. It required speed, and speed was something the seven-year-old boy had in abundance. The object of prisoner was to "capture" members of the opposing team. One day as the neighborhood kids played, Richard caught his brother Manuel. But Manuel broke loose and Richard threw a rock at him to stop him. The rock cut the back of Manuel's head, and he ran home screaming as blood poured from the wound.

When Mr. Gonzales heard what Richard had done, he took his son to the garage and beat him with an electric cord. Then he tied a string to each of Richard's thumbs and pulled his arms upward until they were straight over his head. He attached the strings to the ceiling of the garage and left Richard standing like that for three hours.[1]

This kind of punishment would be considered abusive by today's standards. Most psychologists believe that abused children treat others with force and aggression.[2]

Mr. Gonzales, however, did not feel that he was being abusive. He felt he was being strict. He thought he needed to use these methods to discipline a rebellious son. Furthermore, Richard was the oldest child and Mr. Gonzales thought he must be an example to the younger children.[3] For this reason, Richard suffered through many harsh punishments in his childhood.

But Richard and his father also had good times together. Mr. Gonzales taught his seven-year-old son how to shoot marbles. Marbles is played by flicking a large marble at several smaller ones that have been placed inside a circle. The object is to knock more small marbles outside the circle than one's opponent.

Richard and Mr. Gonzales competed fiercely at marbles, both of them very serious about winning. Richard practiced constantly and before long, he was beating his father. Mr. Gonzales then enlarged the playing circle to make it more difficult for his son to win. Undaunted, Richard practiced more.

Richard played marbles at school, too. But after a while there was no one left in his third-grade class to conquer. So every recess Richard climbed over the fence that separated the younger pupils from the older ones. There he challenged the fourth, fifth, and sixth graders to marbles. He frequently won.

Seeking out more competition, Richard entered local marble tournaments that were held at various Los Angeles parks. He and a friend often rode their home-made scooters to these contests. While on their way to one, Richard accidentally pushed his scooter in front of a moving car. The car's door handle smashed into his face and ripped his left cheek open. An ambulance rushed Richard to the hospital, where he was stitched up. Two weeks later he was back in the neighborhood playing—only now he had a large scar on his left cheek in the shape of an H.[4]

This accident did not prevent Richard from attending more marble tournaments, though. He even won the Los Angeles city championship once. Besides the thrill of competition, Richard went to these tournaments to watch a man who gave exhibitions there. The man was an excellent marble shooter with a jovial personality. But what made him truly extraordinary was the fact that he had no arms. He shot marbles by lying on his side and using his toes. Watching this man convinced Richard that "no matter how bad things got at home, [life] could be worse and [he] could overcome anything."[5]

In addition to this developing determination to rise above all obstacles, Richard was bright. He was a quick learner and his grades were excellent. He liked school and never missed a day of elementary school. Richard even went to school when he was sick because he did not want to stay in bed. Due to his intelligence and excellent attendance, Richard was allowed to skip fourth grade. In 1937 he moved directly from third grade to fifth.

In junior high, Richard joined his school football and basketball teams. He did well on both. Mrs. Gonzales, however, worried that her active son would get hurt. When twelve-year-old Richard asked her for a bicycle, she told him that they were too dangerous and that she would get him something safer.

Richard received a tennis racket for Christmas that year. Mrs. Gonzales had purchased it at a discount store for fifty cents. In addition to diverting Richard from rough games, she hoped the gift would expose him to some of the finer things in life.

At the time, Los Angeles had one of the best private tennis facilities in the West, the Los Angeles Tennis Club. This club was a fancy place, complete with a restaurant, bar, locker rooms, and two professional players to give lessons. Mr. and Mrs. Gonzales could not afford to send Richard to the Los Angeles Tennis Club to learn the game. But even if they had been rich, he would not have been admitted because he was a Mexican American and his skin was too dark. The club had a policy of only admitting white people. Actually, Mr. and Mrs. Gonzales could not afford tennis lessons for Richard anywhere. So he set out to learn the game himself.

Every day Richard walked to a public park where he watched people play tennis. He listened and observed carefully, trying to make sense of the rules. At times he wondered if he would ever figure out the game's confusing scoring system.

A tennis match is really a series of several games. Both players begin at zero, a score that is called love. Each game consists of four points: 15, 30, 40, and game point. The same player serves an entire game, and when the score is announced, the server's score is always said first. When one player misses a ball, the other player earns a point. The first player to reach the game point wins the game. But each game must be won by at least two points. For example, if both players win three points the score is tied at 40–40. This is called deuce. To win this game, a player must earn two consecutive points.

When one game is finished, it is the other player's turn to serve. The player who wins six games first wins that set of games. But a set must also be won by two games. Therefore, a final set score of 6–5 would make it necessary to play at least one more game. When both players are evenly skilled, a set can continue for a long time with the lead alternating after every game.

Tennis was first played at private clubs for the wealthy, such as Newport Casino in Newport, Rhode Island. Many of these clubs discriminated against people of nonwhite ethnic heritage.

Today most tournaments have tie-breaking games to bring a quicker finish to this kind of a set.

Yet the end of a set is still not the end of a tennis contest. Tennis matches consist of a predetermined number of sets. Players most often compete for the best of three sets or the best of five sets.

Richard learned these rules by watching and listening. He was not the only person to learn tennis this way. Most other Mexican Americans and African

Americans had to learn the game on their own, too. This was partly because of poverty, but mostly because of discrimination. The vast majority of lessons were taught at private clubs. These, like the Los Angeles Tennis Club, did not allow people of color to join no matter how much money they had. But this did not keep Richard from playing tennis.

Each day after school, Richard walked to the nearby high school to watch the tennis team practice. There he made friends with a team member named Charles Pate. Pate called Richard "Pancho," a nickname that Richard did not mind when it came from his friend.

Soon Richard was helping Pate with his morning newspaper route. In exchange, Pate gave Richard tennis lessons. Pate taught Richard how to hit forehand and backhand shots. He showed him how to serve a ball. Richard supplemented Pate's instructions by studying the best players and trying to imitate them. As he did, he began developing a style that would mark his tennis game for the rest of his life.

One of the first skills Richard developed was a hard serve. On each serve, a player has two chances to hit the ball over the net and into the correct area of an opponent's court. A player's first missed serve is called a fault. The second one is called a double fault. A double fault gives the opponent a point. When a player serves the ball so hard that a player cannot even make contact with it, the server is said to have aced the opponent. Richard's serves became the hardest around, and he often aced other players. Even when he did not ace them, he rarely faulted on the first serve. A double fault by Richard was practically nonexistent.

Furthermore, Richard was quick. He could move across a tennis court faster than other players. His large size gave him an added advantage in covering ground. Richard would eventually grow six feet three inches tall. As a youth, he had a good start. With a longer stride and longer reach than many other young people, Richard could return shots other players did not have time to retrieve.

It did not take Richard long to wear out the nylon strings in his first racket. Within a month of receiving the gift, he was repairing it with pliers, nails, and new string.[6] His handiwork extended the life of his first racket, enabling him to enter the city's public tennis tournaments. Soon Richard was carrying a first-place ribbon home to his proud mother.

Richard's father was not as excited. Mr. Gonzales believed that tennis was a sport for the idle rich. As far as he was concerned, tennis had no place in Richard's life. It would not help him succeed or earn money.[7] In one way, Mr. Gonzales was right. At the time, very few people earned a living by playing tennis. Those who did were the world's best players and came from wealthy homes or had wealthy sponsors.

Perhaps Richard's father was thinking of another obstacle—racism. Racism was something Richard still did not know much about. His young life revolved around his home, neighborhood, and school. The people in these settings were mostly Mexican American and, therefore, there was no ethnic discrimination. As an adult, Richard explained that he had a sheltered childhood and that his family "didn't try to climb any racial fences."[8]

Even though Richard claimed to be unaware of prejudice against Mexican Americans, it did exist. For example, some Los Angeles swimming pools only admitted Mexican Americans on certain days, and entire neighborhoods barred Mexican Americans from moving into them.[9]

Yet Mr. and Mrs. Gonzales rarely spoke about racism with their children. Instead, they taught them to be proud of their heritage. One brother later remembered how his parents had told their children, "You're Mexican. You want to walk with your head high."[10]

In fact, when Richard first became aware of discrimination, it puzzled him. He could not understand why someone would judge him because of his heritage. He asked his grandmother about the strange concept. She told Richard that he had been lucky to escape discrimination in his young life. But, she went on, someday it would appear. "Perhaps when you ask for a job," she said, "or the look in a policeman's

22

eyes . . . the glances in the stores. It is worse in the heat of anger. When someone denounces you—calls you a Mexican and makes it sound ugly."[11]

Richard's grandmother offered him some advice. She told him to remain calm whenever anyone insulted him. Then, she said, he should imagine that person in his or her underwear. This mental image would make Richard laugh and the hateful words would sting less. It would be years before Richard used her advice. But when he did, he found it worked.

In the meantime, Richard played tennis on Los Angeles's public courts. One of his favorite places was Exposition Park. This park had eight hard-surfaced courts where many Mexican Americans and African Americans played. There was also a tennis shop at the park. It was called the Olympic Tennis Shop, and was run by Frank Poulain. Poulain soon noticed something special about Richard's tennis abilities.

Poulain was not the only one. A sales representative from an athletic supply company once saw Richard play and gave him two new rackets as free samples. Richard was thrilled with the gift, and he tried the rackets out immediately, accidentally staying out an hour past his curfew. When he arrived home that night Mr. Gonzales was furious. He slapped Richard across the face and pulled him upstairs by an ear. Then he threw Richard onto the floor and beat him with a belt.

Throughout the beating, Richard hugged his new rackets to his chest to protect them.

"When I tell you to be home at a certain time you will be home!" his father raged. "If you think you are going to do what you please, you will be taught a lesson! You live in my house and you will do what I say! Tennis is for bums! You will not be a bum! Give me those!"[12]

Before Richard could stop him, Mr. Gonzales pried a racket loose and broke it over his knee. "Go ahead!" Richard screamed in defiance. "Break the other! I'll be back with two more!"[13] The boy was true to his word. When the salesman heard what had happened he gave Richard another racket to replace the broken one.

Early in high school, Richard gave up all other sports to concentrate on tennis. The sport fit him well. There was no standing around between plays like there was in football; no one to throw the ball to as in basketball. Tennis was nothing but pure action. It had to be won by one strong, quick, and smart player. Simply, the sport was tailor-made for Richard.

During his school lunch break, Richard often went outside to practice tennis. One day he stayed outside the whole afternoon working on his various shots. That day's hooky playing was the beginning of a pattern.

Soon Richard was spending more time on the tennis court than in the classroom. Then he was dodging truant officers that the school sent out to find him. As an adult, he once said that he covered more ground running from school officials than he did playing in a tennis tournament.

Not surprisingly, Richard's attendance habits did not sit well with his father. Schooling, not tennis, Mr. Gonzales insisted, was the road to success. So Richard pursued his passion alone. This included finding his own way to tournaments. Usually he rode his bicycle. Looking back, an adult Gonzalez reported that this had been a terrific way to train. "[I] didn't have to worry about my legs being in shape," he once said. "I'd ride all over the city. I'd go 15 to 20 miles a day and not give it a thought."[14]

While Richard traveled from one public court to another, a talented youngster named Herbert Flam was fine-tuning his own tennis game at the Los Angeles Tennis Club. Throughout 1942, Flam was considered the best young player in southern California. In fact, many people thought Flam just might be the hottest youth in the country.

Flam and Richard met for the first time on the court in 1943. While many people knew Flam, few had heard of Richard Gonzalez. Even fewer expected the Mexican-American youth to win. But he did!

By the end of 1943, Richard was ranked the number one boy tennis player in southern California. Just as important as being ranked number one, though, was being noticed by Perry Jones.

Jones's official job title was secretary and tournament manager of the Southern California Amateur Tennis Association. Unofficially, Jones was known for finding and developing talented young tennis players in southern California. Jones was so good at nurturing new players that some people referred to the Southern California Amateur Tennis Association as "Perry Jones's tennis factory."

Jones had the power to make or break a young tennis player. He decided whether or not a certain youngster had enough talent to receive help from the association. The youths that Jones deemed deserving received the best coaching available and were invited to the most prestigious tournaments. The very best were sent on tours around the country to compete. Up until Richard's 1943 victory over Flam, Flam had been Jones's most promising future star. Now Jones turned his attention to Richard.

Jones offered Richard the association's support, giving Richard the chance of a lifetime. There was only one problem. Jones had high expectations for his young tennis players. Not only must they work hard on the court, he expected them to behave off the court as well. This meant getting good grades at school and being model students. Therefore, playing for Jones required a signed statement from a boy's principal saying that he was doing well at school. The only way

Richard would come up with such a statement was through forgery. That was not his style.

Consequently, Jones soon learned of Richard's attendance habits. He promptly told Richard that he must attend school. If he did not, he would be ineligible to play in association tournaments. Some people felt that Jones was being particularly severe with Richard because he was Mexican American. Even Richard believed he was being discriminated against.[15] But Jones denied these charges saying, "It isn't fair for [Richard] to practice tennis all day while the other youngsters are in school."[16] He added that if Richard returned to school as a serious student, he would be welcomed back.

Richard tried. But his heart was not in it. It was not that the work was too difficult or that he had a hard time learning. He just did not want other people telling him what to do.

Richard soon learned he did not have a choice. In 1943 he was sent to a juvenile correctional school because of his truancy and a petty theft.[17] There were no tennis courts at the school and no time to play, anyway. His days were filled with classes and work.

Richard was released from the school in 1944. Though he was only sixteen years old and had only completed tenth grade, he decided to quit school. His friends told him this was a bad idea. His mother pleaded with him to finish high school. Mr. Gonzales forbid him to drop out. Richard quit anyway.

True to his word, Jones crossed Richard off his list of youngsters to receive the association's support. Now Richard was without the backing of the most influential junior tennis program in the region. Such a banishment would have brought an end to most teenagers' dreams of tennis glory. But Richard was not like most young people.

CHAPTER THREE

CLIMBING

 On his own with no one else's rules, Richard saw opportunity. Now he could spend all of his time playing tennis. When he was not on the court, he was in the Olympic Tennis Shop talking about the sport with Frank Poulain.

But soon the reality of Richard's situation began to sink in. Because he would not go to school, he could not compete in prestigious tournaments and gain recognition beyond Los Angeles's public courts. Further scrapes with the law might land him back in a juvenile detention facility. This too, meant no tennis. In an effort to escape his predicament, Richard enlisted in the United States Navy in the fall of 1945.[1]

Gonzalez spent most of the next year and a half on a transport ship on the Pacific Ocean. He was assigned to maintenance tasks such as scrubbing the ship's deck. Gonzalez did not like the Navy. All of its rules and regulations reminded him of school. Worse still, Gonzalez could not play tennis. As soon as he was discharged in January 1947, he returned to his home in Los Angeles and his second home at Exposition Park.

Mr. Gonzales told his nineteen-year-old son that he had three choices. He could go to school, get a job, or leave home. Gonzalez packed his clothes and tennis rackets and headed for Poulain's shop. For the next couple of weeks he stayed there, sleeping on a sofa in the back of the store. Finally, Mr. Gonzales resigned himself to his son's determination to play tennis and let him move back home.

While Gonzalez had been floating around the Pacific, his old rival Herbert Flam had been winning tennis tournaments around the country. Flam had even captured the National Junior Championship twice. Area experts believed Flam would place well in an upcoming men's tournament, the Southern California Championships. Jack Kramer, another former student of Perry Jones's, was expected to win the tournament. Kramer, in fact, currently held the United States title.

As for Gonzalez, he had not even received an invitation to the California tournament. This was not surprising. He had only been on the tennis scene for a short while before being suspended because of his poor school attendance. Then he joined the Navy and disappeared for nearly two years. But now Gonzalez was back, and he was about to let the tennis world know it. He promptly sent in an entry blank for the tournament, hoping to be accepted.

When Perry Jones received Gonzalez's application, he was faced with a dilemma. Should he let Gonzalez back into tournament play? The young man was still a high school dropout and apparently had no interest in returning to school. But Gonzalez had been in the Navy, and Jones reasoned that anyone old enough to serve his country was old enough to make his own decision about education. Therefore, based solely on the young man's tennis skills, Jones invited Gonzalez to play in the Southern California Championships. It would be Gonzalez's first men's tournament.

Tennis tournaments proceed through several rounds of play. They are usually single elimination affairs, meaning that as soon as a player loses a match, he is out of the tournament. The winning player advances to the tournament's next round. Once more the losers are eliminated and the winners move on. When only two players are left, the tournament winner is decided by a final match. Before the tournament begins, the best players are seeded (ranked according to their ability). For example, the person who the organizers think will win the tournament is seeded number one. The player who is expected to come in second is seeded number two, and so on. The seeded players are not scheduled to compete against each other until the tournament's last rounds. This keeps them from eliminating each other in the early rounds.

As one of the best players in California, Flam was seeded in the Southern California Championship. Gonzalez was not. However, each day Gonzalez worked his way a little closer to the final round. Match by match he advanced until his name was placed next to Flam's in semifinal action.

On the morning of this important match, Gonzalez stuffed his athletic bag with tennis shoes, a plain white T-shirt, and an old pair of tennis shorts. His mother wished him luck, and he walked out of the house feeling confident. It took Gonzalez three streetcars to get to the elegant Los Angeles Tennis Club, but he arrived in plenty of time. While waiting for his match to begin, he noticed movie stars among the spectators. More important to him, though, were the friends from Exposition Park who had come to cheer him on.[2] Frank Poulain and Chuck Pate were among them.

Gonzalez's friends crowded into the gallery along with several other spectators. Some had been watching Gonzalez in the early rounds of action and were impressed. They predicted that the Gonzalez–Flam match would be an intense contest between two of the best young players on the West Coast. They were not disappointed.

When the first set ended, Flam had beaten Gonzalez, 10–8. But as the match wore on, Flam could not handle Gonzalez's lightning serve, and Gonzalez took the second set, 8–6. With the score tied one set apiece, the winner of the next set would be the winner of the match. Gonzalez won it, 6–4, and the uninvited, unseeded young man knocked the brightest West Coast hopeful out of the tournament.

Now Gonzalez advanced to the final where he would meet Jack Kramer. This time no one expected Gonzalez to win, and he did not. Kramer beat Gonzalez, 6–2, 6–4, 3–6, 6–3. In one sense, though, Gonzalez was victorious. During the contest, he aced Kramer six times. He even beat Kramer in one set, something that only a few players had done all year. Gonzalez was happy with his performance, feeling that he had proven himself to be a top contender in amateur tennis.[3]

Perry Jones agreed. He immediately offered Gonzalez a spot on the association's 1947 tour to the East. This was an expense-paid trip to compete in several tournaments against some of the country's best players. If Gonzalez did well, he could earn national attention. Gonzalez packed his bags because he did not intend to waste this golden opportunity.

Yet the tour was not always easy. First of all, Gonzalez felt like an outsider among most of the players in his California group. He later stated that the more experienced players ignored him but gave advice to other rookies. "I felt that I should have had more support from those guys," he once said.[4] After all, Gonzalez reasoned, they were all representing Southern California. But any strategies Gonzalez picked up were the result of his own astute observation rather than tips from the veterans in the group.

For example, most of the tournaments in the East were held on grass courts. Gonzalez had never played on grass before. So it took him some time to realize that a ball skidded across sod instead of bouncing sharply like it did on concrete. He also had to learn that a ball's bounce on lawn courts was highly unpredictable. To compensate for this, Gonzalez always tried to hit the ball before it bounced on his side of the net.

Being left to learn on his own made Gonzalez resentful.[5] But his tennis did not suffer. Although he did not win any of the tournaments on this first tour, he played well and became more widely known on the national tennis scene. He also made some important new friends. For instance, in New York he met Frank Shields, a tennis champion from the 1930s. Shields

Gonzalez's determination and skill earned him a place on a 1947 tour in the eastern United States.

would give the rookie crucial support in the months ahead.

In addition, Gonzalez turned Perry Jones into an admirer. Jones was impressed by Gonzalez's aggressive style on the court. He was also impressed by Gonzalez's integrity. Once Jones accidentally sent Gonzalez an expense check for ninety-eight dollars too much. Although no one would have known the difference, Gonzalez promptly returned the overpayment. This simple act of honesty endeared Gonzalez to Jones for years to come.[6]

In September 1947, Gonzalez made his first appearance at the United States National Championship in an area of New York City called Forest Hills. The top-seeded player that year was Jack Kramer. Frank Parker was seeded No. 2 and Gardnar Mulloy No. 3. At his premier outing of the United States's most prestigious amateur tournament, Gonzalez played so well that he almost beat Mulloy.

Back in Los Angeles, Gonzalez played in the Pacific Southwest Tournament. There he defeated Jaroslav Drobny, the No. 5 ranked player in the world and Frank Parker, the No. 3 ranked player in the world. This took him to the tournament final where he lost to Jack Kramer—again.

Now Gonzalez was definitely being noticed. But with greater fame came closer scrutiny, and tennis fans could see that Gonzalez was different from other tennis players. First of all, he was not white. Second, he was not the socially sophisticated young man that many people expected tennis players to be. Gonzalez smoked cigarettes and played poker. He stayed out until the wee hours of the morning and enjoyed an occasional beer. At times, he seemed a little too relaxed as he sat courtside waiting to play.

Sports reporters noticed Gonzalez, too. They wrote about his cannonball serve, his dynamite style at the net, and his ability to conquer an opponent. They also reported that Gonzalez had an easygoing, relaxed out-look on training. These comments on Gonzalez's casual attitude may have been a veiled reference to the false stereotype of the "lazy Mexican."

Whether they were or not, Gonzalez started climb-ing that fence of racial barriers his family had always avoided. The tennis elite was predominantly white. Some still did not think a person of color was their equal. These fans and players were unhappy with the prospect of a Mexican American joining their ranks. Gonzalez later reported that it was at this point that he began seeing the subtle but definite edges of racism. For example, he often heard spectators commenting on the deep scar on his cheek, assuming it was caused in a knife fight. According to Gonzalez, many people believed that "a knife scar and a Mexican-American youth go hand in hand."[7]

Other people of color encountered prejudice in tennis, too. African Americans were openly barred from many tournaments, no matter how talented they were. For instance, one African-American youngster named Oscar Johnson had won the Pacific Coast junior title every year from 1946–1948. But at a tournament in St. Louis, he was told he could not play. Johnson and his lawyer challenged the decision and he was finally admitted. Yet excluding African Americans and other minorities from tennis tournaments was a common practice across the United States.[8]

As for Gonzalez, he was never turned away from a tournament because he was Mexican American. But he was not always made to feel welcome, either. Even the Los Angeles Tennis Club still did not admit non-white members. So though Gonzalez played at the club and it was the home of his sponsor, the Southern California Tennis Association, he still was not allowed to become a member.[9]

By the end of 1947, Gonzalez was ranked the seventeenth best player in the United States. He had earned this ranking by playing well in ten different tournaments around the country. Unfortunately, by doing so Gonzalez had again broken some rules. The organization that regulated tennis, the United States Lawn Tennis Association (USLTA), allowed amateur players to accept expense money for only eight invitational tournaments a year. Any more than that would

Gonzalez proved he could play tennis, but his dark skin and unschooled form made him unique among the other champions of the late 1940s.

make a player a professional. This distinction between amateurs and professionals was an important one.

Amateurs were not allowed to make money from tennis. They could not win prizes, endorse products, or teach lessons. The only money amateurs could receive for tennis was the money it cost them to attend tournaments. Professionals, on the other hand, could make money from the sport. They could earn championship purses and be paid to advertise products or coach.

But being a professional had drawbacks, too. Professionals were not allowed to enter the most prestigious tennis tournaments in the world. For example, the four biggest national championships—those of the United States, Great Britain, France, and Australia— were closed to professionals. Furthermore, professionals could not compete in international team contests such as the Davis Cup competition.

Because Gonzalez had played in more invitational tournaments than amateur status allowed, the USLTA board met to decide on his tennis fate. Perry Jones went to the meeting to defend Gonzalez. He described him as a wonderful and dignified young man.[10] Jones convinced the board that an appropriate penalty for Gonzalez would be suspension from tournament play from February to June of 1948. This would keep Gonzalez out of tennis for several months. But because the most important United States tournaments were held after June, Gonzalez would be allowed to participate in these. Of course, Gonzalez did not sit around waiting for his suspension to end. He practiced daily. He also developed a new interest. Her name was Henrietta Pedrin.

Gonzalez first met the seventeen-year-old at one of his sister's parties. The five-foot one-inch, ninety-eight pound beauty made his heart pound. Gonzalez took Henrietta on a date the very next evening, and from then on they were constant companions. Each afternoon

Henrietta watched Gonzalez practice tennis. At night they went dancing. Two months later, Gonzalez asked Henrietta to marry him, and she said yes.

But both knew that their parents would be against the marriage. Henrietta was very young and Gonzalez was supposed to be giving tennis his full attention. So one day in March, the two drove to Arizona where they were married quickly and quietly. They kept their wedding a secret and returned to their parents' homes as if nothing had changed.

Then one day Henrietta's mother decided that her daughter was spending too much time with Gonzalez. When Gonzalez went to pick up Henrietta, Mrs. Pedrin informed him that her daughter was staying home. Gonzalez was so frustrated he let the secret out and told Mrs. Pedrin that he had a right to see his own wife.[11]

The newlyweds moved into a small apartment and lived on expense money Gonzalez had saved from his tennis travels. The money did not go far. So when the Mexican government approached him with a unique offer, he was interested.

Mexican officials wanted Gonzalez to play tennis for Mexico. If he would become a Mexican citizen, he was told, the government would pay for a college education and give Gonzalez money to travel around the world to play tennis. Furthermore, the government would guarantee Gonzalez a lifelong job at the Mexican consulate in Los Angeles.

This was an attractive offer to a young man who knew he wanted to spend his life playing tennis but had no way to finance this dream. Gonzalez thought about the offer for several weeks. Then a friend inadvertently helped him make up his mind. The friend asked Gonzalez if he would rather be on a Mexican or United States Davis Cup team. Suddenly, Gonzalez's answer was crystal clear. There was only one nation he wanted to represent in international play—the United States.[12] The matter was settled.

As soon as his suspension was lifted, Gonzalez was back on the courts. In Chicago, he walked away with the first-place trophy in the national clay court championships. Next he won the state championships of California and New Jersey.

While Gonzalez collected trophies, Jack Kramer made a monumental announcement: He was turning professional. This news sent the amateur world scrambling. With Kramer out of the amateur picture, there were several players capable of winning the 1948 United States title. Richard Gonzalez believed he was one of them.[13]

Throughout the summer, Gonzalez had been watching the other top players closely. He had made mental notes of their weaknesses and filed the information away. He hoped he would get a chance to use it at the national championship in September.

Most people were betting on Ted Schroeder to win the title. Schroeder had won the United States Championship in 1942, and many felt he was reaching his peak. Gonzalez had already lost to Schroeder seven times in various tournaments. According to Gonzalez, Schroeder had some kind of a psychological hold over him. Whenever the two met in a locker room before a match, Schroeder deflated Gonzalez's morale. Gonzalez claimed this made him play poorly. Indeed, Schroeder would be an obstacle to Gonzalez's dreams of glory at Forest Hills.

Then came the news that Schroeder was not entering the nationals because of other obligations. Now Gonzalez was positive he could take the title, even though sixteen other men were ranked above him.

Tennis fans, however, were accustomed to watching their stars grow from childhood. This was only the second season Gonzalez had played in major competition, and to them he was a novice. Talented or not, many believed that it took years for championship players to develop. Few believed that Gonzalez would make it to the final match.

The tournament officials seemed to feel the same. They seeded Gonzalez No. 8. But all of the experts in the world could not dull Gonzalez's dreams. In September he left for Forest Hills, confident that he would return to Los Angeles as the United States amateur tennis champion.

United States Champion

 Gonzalez was on his own at the national tournament. He had no coach to tell him what to do and no trainer to oversee his conditioning. He could practice or not, develop a strategy or not—the choice was his. The only advice he received came from his new friend, Frank Shields. Shields told Gonzalez to play hard for every point. Gonzalez promised he would.

The young man kept his promise. In the quarter-final round he beat the No. 1 seed, Frank Parker. Now Gonzalez advanced to the semifinals where he would meet Jaroslav Drobny. The other semifinal match was between Eric Sturgess from South Africa and Herbert Flam. Gonzalez believed that he could beat Flam if the two met in final action.[1] But first Gonzalez went out to meet Drobny.

Drobny played well and Gonzalez lost the first set, 10–8. Then, in what one writer called a dazzling exhibition of speed and power, Gonzalez won the next three sets to win the match. In the meantime, Sturgess beat Flam to set up the final round of action—Richard Gonzalez against Eric Sturgess.

Spectators packed the stands at Forest Hills on September 19, 1948, eager to witness the Gonzalez–Sturgess match. Gonzalez stepped onto the court hungry for victory. He took the first set, 6–2. Then he won the second set, 6–3. Gonzalez and Sturgess exchanged leads several times in the third set until the score was 13–12, Gonzalez. As evening descended on the court, the officials decided it was getting too dark to play. They told Gonzalez and Sturgess that they could play one more game. If this did not decide the contest, the match would be finished the next day. A proverb flashed through Gonzalez's mind: Never put off until tomorrow what you can do today. Gonzalez won the next game to claim the third set—and the United States National Championship!

Suddenly, Richard Gonzalez was the most popular tennis player in the nation. Articles about him appeared in *The New York Times* newspaper and in

Time and *Life* magazines. Each one emphasized that no one had *ever* risen to the top so quickly. As Allison Danzig put it, "The rankest outsider of modern times sits on the tennis throne today."[2]

Gonzalez was unique in other ways, too. He had a distinctive playing style that many writers compared to a jungle cat. He crouched low in preparation for his opponent's hits. When one came, he pounced on the ball with great fury. But the one aspect of Gonzalez's game that received the most attention was his serve. Enthusiasts often described it as a rocket.

In addition, Gonzalez created excitement among spectators. For years, tennis fans had been watching the same players compete against each other in matches that had become routine. But no one could tell what would happen in a Gonzalez match. Wondering if he would make an inexplicable error or hit a brilliant shot, people leaned forward in their seats to watch him play. Gonzalez himself called his game unpredictable. "Sometimes my forehand is my weakness," he explained, and "sometimes my backhand. It all depends on how I'm feeling that day."[3]

Fans also found the new champion's background intriguing. Some writers characterized him as rebellious and emphasized his truancy during high school. This soon earned him the title of the bad boy of tennis. In a world so long populated by well-mannered, properly schooled young men, Gonzalez became characterized as a rebel from a poor Mexican-American family. Some writers called him the kid from "the other side of the tracks." Gonzalez felt that this description was an exaggeration of the working-class home in which he grew up.[4] But the image stuck—possibly because so many people found it fascinating.

Furthermore, Gonzalez emanated a charisma that drew people to him. He was confident and easygoing on the court. He was also handsome, and many writers noted that groups of young ladies often came to watch Gonzalez play.

Finally, Gonzalez was the first nonwhite person to win the national title, and his Mexican heritage interested many people. Some reporters emphasized it by calling him Pancho, Chuck Pate's nickname for his friend. But the name felt different coming from the press, and Gonzalez hated it.[5] Pancho was a name some non-Hispanics used to address a Hispanic man without bothering to learn his name. It sometimes referred to a person of low social status. Many Mexican Americans, in fact, considered the nickname to be a racial slur.

It reminded Gonzalez of the negative stereotype people had of Mexican Americans. This stereotype portrayed Mexicans as stupid and lazy. Indeed, writers continued reporting that Gonzalez had a lackadaisical approach to life and tennis. One wrote, "Next to eating Mexican food, the thing California-born Richard A. [Gonzalez] probably enjoys more than anything else is

After he won the National Championship in 1948, Gonzalez rose to fame. Many tennis fans were charmed by his intensity on the court and by his good looks.

taking life easy. When the mood hits him, 'Pancho' plays tennis . . ."[6] Given the negative connotations of the name Pancho, Gonzalez wanted to be called Richard.

No matter what people called him, though, people did call. Suddenly Gonzalez was in demand for radio, newspaper, and magazine interviews. His social calendar filled with parties and dinners in his honor. He became a frequent guest in the homes of wealthy tennis fans. But Gonzalez usually felt out of place at these functions. He much preferred the company of his old friends at Exposition Park.[7]

In fact, Gonzalez still frequented the Olympic Tennis Shop and played pickup games with his friends there. Some people commented that this habit would ruin Gonzalez's game. Many did not see Gonzalez as a true champion, anyway. They believed that if Schroeder had entered the 1948 nationals, he would have beaten Gonzalez. Consequently, Gonzalez felt he had something to prove when he was pitted against Schroeder in the Pacific Southwest Tournament that fall.

Gonzalez stepped up to the task in front of a capacity crowd at the Los Angeles Tennis Club—and failed. Schroeder beat Gonzalez 6–3, 4–6, 7–5, and 10–8 in the tournament semifinal. In Gonzalez's words, Schroeder "showed no respect at all for the new crown that had been placed on my head."[8]

There would soon be joy in Gonzalez's life, though. In January, Henrietta gave birth to a baby boy. The

Gonzalezes named their new son Richard Alonzo, Jr. Between fatherhood and socializing, Gonzalez found little time for training. By the end of the month he had gained twenty-five pounds. The added weight hurt his tennis game.

In February both Gonzalez and Schroeder entered another California tournament. Gonzalez looked forward to one more chance to prove he deserved the national title. Then, on the day before the match, Gonzalez's partner in a doubles game accidentally smashed him in the face with his racket. The blow broke Gonzalez's nose. Gonzalez, however, was determined to keep his appointment with Schroeder. He arrived at the court the next day with a bandaged nose. Although he had to breathe out of his mouth, he managed to beat Schroeder 6–2, 6–8, and 9–7. Gonzalez later said he would happily break his nose every day of the week if it meant playing that well.[9]

In May Gonzalez faced Schroeder again at the Southern California Tennis Championships. This time Schroeder won in less than forty minutes. One observer noted that the contest was over before Gonzalez even warmed up. Four days later, Gonzalez played at the French National Championship in Paris. He lost there, too.

By June Gonzalez was again feeling that he needed to prove himself worthy of the United States Championship. Wimbledon, the national championship

50

of Great Britain, loomed ahead. This was thought of as the most important amateur tennis title of all. Even so, Gonzalez continued to turn down offers of instruction from the best coaches around, people who might help him gain consistency with his shots. "My game has to be careless," Gonzalez said, defending his decision. "That's the way it's built."[10]

But the tension was mounting. Schroeder and other world-class players would be at Wimbledon. Even Gonzalez's mother noticed an uncharacteristic seriousness in her son as the tournament approached. "Something is happening to Richard," she said. "When he [had] his picture taken for the passport, I [asked] the photographer to take four extra pictures. In only one picture was he smiling. He is not so happy any more playing tennis. I do not like that."[11] One writer put it another way, "Gonzalez knows he *must* win at Wimbledon, and the knowledge is forcing him, somewhat against his will, to grow up."[12]

In late June 1949, Richard Gonzalez walked onto a Wimbledon court for the first time in his life. In light of his numerous losses that year, he was seeded second. Schroeder was honored with the No. 1 spot. This seeding predicted a final match between Gonzalez and Schroeder. But Gonzalez never made it past the third round of play. He was eliminated there by an Australian named Geoff Brown. Schroeder, on the other hand, won his way to the final where he beat Drobny for the Wimbledon title.

Gonzalez and Parker did manage to beat Mulloy and Schroeder in Wimbledon's doubles championship. Another victory came in August when Gonzalez played on the Davis Cup team and beat two Australian players to help keep the trophy in United States possession. These two wins boosted Gonzalez's morale, and by autumn he felt ready to win the national championship again.[13]

Others were not as confident. After reviewing his erratic record, more and more came to believe that Gonzalez's 1948 victory had been a combination of luck and Schroeder's absence from the match. Because of this, one sportswriter called Gonzalez the greatest "cheese champion" in tennis history, meaning that Gonzalez had won the title in a cheesy or cheap way.[14] Now Gonzalez was dubbed with another nickname he detested—"Gorgo," short for Gorgonzola cheese.

Schroeder showed up at Forest Hills still elated from his victory at Wimbledon. Experts felt that the tournament's final match would be another Gonzalez–Schroeder showdown. Most favored Schroeder. But these forecasters did not know how much being called the "cheese champion" hurt Gonzalez. Nor did they know how determined this pain made him.

Something else motivated Gonzalez. A man named Bobby Riggs was looking for new talent. Riggs was the promoter of the most prestigious professional tennis tour in the world. Every year he hired a few of the best players to compete against each other in cities all over the globe. At the time, Riggs was looking for someone to challenge his latest star, Jack Kramer. Many people assumed that Riggs would ask the winner of the 1949 United States Nationals to turn pro. His touring contract could be worth as much as $75,000.

This thought energized Gonzalez.[15] Being a top-ranked amateur was a career that needed full-time attention. It meant hours of daily training and frequent trips away from home for tournaments. These commitments made it almost impossible for a serious amateur to hold a regular job. Most amateurs, therefore, had to rely on other sources of income to pay their living expenses.

But Gonzalez had no other sources of income. "As an amateur," he later reported, "I saved enough from the expense money I received to be able to practice and play occasionally in the off season . . . I just managed to get by when I was out of competition, but I had to scrape."[16]

Gonzalez now had a family to support. Earning money was a necessity and doing it by playing tennis would be a dream come true. At Forest Hills the tournament officials seeded Schroeder first and Gonzalez second. Both men won their early rounds of play and advanced to the final. As Gonzalez readied himself for the 1949 championship match, he knew he was playing for more than a title—he was playing for a dream.

PAST TENSE

 It took a record-breaking thirty-four games for Schroeder to beat Gonzalez in the first set. But Gonzalez was not about to give up. He continued his battle for every point until he faced Schroeder in a final fifth set. When Gonzalez captured the match-winning point, the crowd went wild.

Most had been cheering for Gonzalez as the game progressed. Some were impressed by his lightning serve and powerful shots. But more than anything else, people sensed and respected Gonzalez's resolve to win. As Danzig reported in the next day's newspaper,

Gonzalez showed outstanding perseverance, moral fiber, and good sportsmanship.[1]

As for Gonzalez, he was happy to shed the title of "cheese champion." He later reported that the best part of winning was appearing on the next cover of a magazine called *American Lawn Tennis*.[2] Appropriately, the caption read "The Last Laugh."

On September 20, 1949, Gonzalez turned professional. He signed a contract to become a part of Bobby Riggs's 1950 tennis tour. Gonzalez would play against Jack Kramer for a guaranteed salary of $60,000. The winner of the most matches at the end of the tour would be considered the professional champion.

Some experts felt that Gonzalez was too inexperienced to turn pro. But financial realities made the move logical to Gonzalez. Henrietta was about to have another baby. Soon Gonzalez would have two children and a wife to support. Furthermore, he was full of optimism and confident about his own tennis skills. So he packed his bags and bade his family good-bye.

Now several nights each week Gonzalez laced up his shoes to face Jack Kramer. Although his opponent never changed, the city where they played always did. From Boston to Chicago to Memphis, Tennessee, Gonzalez and Kramer traversed the United States by car. At each destination they played a three-set match, often on a canvas-covered court that traveled with them. After each match, Gonzalez unwound with a leisurely steak dinner. In the morning, he packed his bags and rackets and hopped into his car to drive to the next stop. Gonzalez found this lifestyle draining.[3] But no matter how he felt, the tennis match always went on. One night Gonzalez reported that he had sprained an ankle and could not play. "What do you mean—can't play?" Kramer asked him. "We always play."[4] Gonzalez received a shot of Novocain for his pain and hit the court.

Gonzalez was also learning about the intensity of competition on the pro tour. Kramer was a merciless opponent who never let up even when he was several points ahead. Gonzalez later said that Kramer was one of the toughest competitors he had ever faced. But this did not discourage him. In fact, the high level of competition inspired Gonzalez. Most notably, he saw the value of Kramer's killer instinct and developed one of his own. Gonzalez once observed, "Most [players] would crush their poor old mothers, 6–0, if she stood in the path of a championship."[5]

Kramer used winning tactics off the court, too. For example, knowing that Gonzalez loved soft drinks, he arranged to have an ice-cold soda waiting for him at every stop. Kramer was not being kind, though. He believed that soft drinks were unhealthy and would weaken an athlete. By providing Gonzalez with one, he hoped to gain a slight edge over him by game time.[6]

Kramer did not need any extra edges. He trounced Gonzalez night after night. Each loss was painful to Gonzalez because it represented a threat to his livelihood. The winning player on this tour would be asked back the next year. The loser had no such guarantee. By the tour's end, Kramer had beaten Gonzalez ninety-six matches to twenty-seven. Even so, Gonzalez had made more than $70,000.

Money, however, could not mend Gonzalez's broken ego. Nor could it guarantee Gonzalez a future in pro tennis. A grim Gonzalez headed back to Los Angeles, hoping that Riggs would find a place for him on the 1951 tour. He did not.

Richard Gonzalez was only twenty-one years old when Bobby Riggs told him he was "past tense." As Riggs so bluntly put it, "You came, you saw—and Jack Kramer conquered."[7] Then Riggs offered Gonzalez the faintest glimmer of hope. He advised Gonzalez to stay in shape and play in all of the professional tournaments he could. If he proved he was still a top competitor, he might get another chance on a future tour.

Soon the next year's touring players were announced. The invincible Jack Kramer would meet Francisco Segura, a player from Ecuador. Segura, like Gonzalez, had been nicknamed Pancho because of his Hispanic heritage. As Kramer and Segura headed off to play tennis, Gonzalez stayed behind to hit balls off the wall of his garage.

On his first professional tennis tour in 1950, Gonzalez faced Jack Kramer in 123 matches. Gonzalez lost all but twenty-seven of them.

Gonzalez missed tennis. He also missed the intensity of constant competition. Looking for an activity to replace tennis, he took up golf. It bored him.

Then he tried gambling. Night after night Gonzalez drove to poker parlors outside of Los Angeles, where he matched wits with experienced gamblers. The high stakes for which they played provided the excitement Gonzalez craved. Unfortunately, he usually lost and before long finances forced him to find a different hobby.

Next Gonzalez turned to car racing, something he had always enjoyed. Henrietta objected to her husband's latest pastime because of its danger. She urged him to think of his family. Gonzalez now had two more sons—Michael and Danny—to care for.[8] But Gonzalez told Henrietta that the constant fear of death hanging over his head was just what he needed to take his mind off professional tennis.

Racing was not the only thing that Gonzalez and Henrietta argued about. While his tennis career collapsed, Gonzalez's marriage seemed to be deteriorating, too. Gonzalez moved out of his home in March 1952. For the next three years, he would live in a variety of apartments, later saying that home was wherever he kept his tennis rackets. Even though he was not playing professionally, tennis still drove his life.

When the Olympic Tennis Shop was put up for sale, it seemed natural for Gonzalez to buy it. For several months, he operated the little store where he had spent so many hours as a teen. When business was slow he played a set or two, often with Oscar Johnson. Johnson gave Gonzalez a good workout.

Occasionally Gonzalez played tennis at the Los Angeles Tennis Club. But few players there were much competition. Remembering Riggs's advice, Gonzalez entered whatever professional tournaments he could. The most important of these was the World's Professional Championship held in a suburb of Cleveland, Ohio. This tournament is often referred to as the United States Professional Championship.[9] In 1952 Gonzalez made it to the final round of the tournament where he faced Kramer's latest vanquished opponent, Francisco Segura. Although Segura could not beat Kramer, he did beat Gonzalez. However, the match was very close.

Gonzalez was back in Cleveland for the Professional Championship in 1953. This time he won the tournament by beating Don Budge. By now Bobby Riggs had retired as the promoter of the tennis tour, and Jack Kramer had retired from competition to take Riggs's place.

Kramer's retirement made way for a new professional tennis champion. As the newest promoter, he promptly offered contracts to four of the men he thought most capable of filling his shoes: Francisco Segura, Frank Sedgman, Don Budge, and Richard

Gonzalez. Now, three years after his devastating debut on the pro tour, Gonzalez was back.

Kramer's 1954 tour would be different from the previous man-to-man tours. It would be a round-robin tour in which the four players continually changed opponents among themselves. The winners of one night's matches would play each other the following

$\mathbf{G}$onzalez (right) proved he was still a top contender by winning the 1953 World's Professional Tennis Championship held in Cleveland, Ohio.

night. Likewise, the losers would face off. The man who won the most matches at the end of the tour would be declared the new professional tennis champion. Although each player received the same pay whether he won or lost, Gonzalez knew that for him especially, the stakes for winning this tour were enormous. Losing might bring a permanent end to his tennis career.

Each of the four men on the tour was able and fierce. But Gonzalez beat them all. As if to emphasize his worthiness, he also won the 1954 Professional Championship in Cleveland.

That same year Gonzalez's parents were divorced. His father remarried shortly afterward. As for Gonzalez, he moved back home in March 1955. He and Henrietta had decided to give their marriage another chance. Gonzalez was thrilled with their reconciliation and glad to be living with his sons again. Richard, Jr., helped his father tinker with his race cars. He also played tennis with him, and Gonzalez claimed his son already showed talent.

Although there was no pro tour in 1955, Gonzalez won the professional title in Cleveland again. That same year Spalding Sports began selling a tennis racket named after and signed by Gonzalez. This was the beginning of a long relationship. Gonzalez would help design and sign Spalding rackets for the next twenty-five years.

PANCHO GONZALES
Autograph
T E N N I S   R A C K E T

The Most Playable Championship Racket In Tennis!

* Superb six-ply Belgian White Ash Frames — powerful, tough, resilient.

* Special extra taut multi-filament Nylon strings.

* Each racket individually weighed and balanced to exacting specifications.

* Complete range of weights and grip sizes for every player preference.

SELECT SPALDING CONFIDENTLY

PANCHO GONZALES AUTOGRAPH
The world's No. 1 Championship racket — first choice of top players the world over. Superb six-ply White Ash Frame with rounded white Ash overlays. Rawhide reinforcement outside shoulders, white fiber inside. Special multi-filament braided Nylon strings, precision strung by machine for extra tautness, absolute uniformity between each and every string. All string holes carefully grooved or countersunk. Fibre-Welded throat. Premium grade perforated Tan leather grip with Gold center stripe.
Grip Sizes and Weights: 4½" Light or Medium; 4⅝" Light or Medium; 4¾" Medium or Heavy; 4⅞" Medium (frame only).

52-204	Multi-Filament Nylon Strings	$24.00 Each
52-104	Frame Only	$20.50 Each

60

Throughout the 1950s, Richard Gonzalez's name was synonymous with championship tennis. For many years, Spalding Sports manufactured a "Pancho Gonzales" signature racket. Back in 1965, the top of the line cost twenty-four dollars.

During 1955 a man named Tony Trabert ruled the amateur tennis world. Trabert had won three of the four major national championships that year—France, Great Britain, and the United States. Soon after winning the United States title, he turned professional by signing a contract with Jack Kramer. He would be pitted against Gonzalez in Kramer's 1956 tour.

Gonzalez was happy to be competing regularly again. But the financial arrangements of this tour angered him. Trabert was guaranteed earnings of $75,000. Gonzalez, however, was promised only $15,000.[10] This seemed terribly unfair, and Gonzalez went to Kramer for an explanation.

Kramer told Gonzalez that the tour's profits depended on how many people came to watch the matches. If people liked Gonzalez, they would come and the tour would make a lot of money. If people did not like him, no one would come. Because Kramer did not know how the public would react to Gonzalez, he was a financial risk. This, Kramer said, was why Gonzalez's salary was so low.

Frustrated, Gonzalez trained harder than ever. He lost weight and sharpened his volley. He improved his already powerful serve. When he saw Trabert he told him, "You'd better get used to losing."[11] Trabert had little choice.

By March, Gonzalez was leading Trabert thirty-four matches to eleven. When the tour ended, Gonzalez had conquered Trabert seventy-four matches to twenty-four. And though Trabert lost his spot on the professional tour, he praised Gonzalez's tennis. "Gonzalez is the greatest natural athlete tennis has ever known," he said. "The way he can move that 6-foot-3-inch frame of his around the court is almost unbelievable. He instinctively does the right thing at the right time. Doesn't even have to stop to think."[12]

In 1956 Gonzalez won the United States Professional Tournament for the fourth straight year. He also won England's prestigious professional championship. His serve continued to be his greatest strength, and it was once clocked at 112 miles per hour. This was the fastest serve among the pros.

An Australian named Ken Rosewall became Gonzalez's opponent for the 1957 tour. Gonzalez won the first match, and kept on winning. By the time the two had played sixty matches, Gonzalez had won forty of them.

In fact, Gonzalez was so good that some fans seemed bored with the tour. Fearing that a loss of interest would mean a loss in profit, Kramer called Gonzalez into his office one day and asked him to take it easy on Rosewall. Although Kramer did not want Gonzalez to actually lose matches on purpose, he asked Gonzalez to let Rosewall stay close enough to maintain a little excitement. Reluctantly, Gonzalez agreed.

During the 1957 tour, Jack Kramer feared that a lack of fans would lead to a loss of profit. Today, in addition to money from ticket sales, tours like the Citibank Champions (pictured) get corporate sponsors to help make a profit.

Shortly after their talk, though, Gonzalez was back in Kramer's office saying that giving up points was ruining his concentration. Kramer understood and realized that his request had been unreasonable. He told Gonzalez to forget their deal.[13]

When the Gonzalez–Rosewall tour ended, Gonzalez had beaten him fifty matches to twenty-six. Gonzalez was clearly the new king of professional tennis. Another reporter put it more colorfully, saying that Gonzalez had clearly "emerged from the bloody free-for-all with Jack Kramer's abandoned crown clenched in his predatory jaws."[14]

"FIFTY POINTS ON TERROR"

By 1958 Richard Gonzalez was known everywhere as the best tennis player in the world. But in addition to his reputation for great tennis, he had developed a reputation for his personality. When Gonzalez first stepped into the public spotlight, he had been described as charismatic and confident. But as the years progressed, some people came to see this self-assuredness as conceit.

These people's opinions were not improved by Gonzalez's curt treatment of his fans. He regularly refused to sign autographs before matches, which made some fans feel he was mean-spirited and haughty. Gonzalez defended his actions by saying that he had to conserve his energy for competition. Besides, he said, he was usually preoccupied with tactical thoughts before his matches. But Gonzalez did sign autographs *after* many matches—especially victorious ones.

Gonzalez was also criticized for the outspoken manner in which he questioned calls he did not like. He became known for the icy glares and sarcastic remarks he directed at officials. For example, after a call went against him, he might turn to the crowd and ask, "Is there an eye doctor about?"[1]

Many incidents were more confrontational. During one match, Gonzalez was particularly hot and a heckler kept offending him. After several catcalls, Gonzalez demanded that the heckler show his face. He did not. Then, as Gonzalez prepared to serve a game-winning point, the heckler shouted again to distract him. Gonzalez stopped for a moment to regain his concentration. When he served, he double faulted and went on to lose the game. While walking to the other side of the court, Gonzalez took an angry swing at a microphone standing next to the court and sent it flying.[2]

Another time Gonzalez was battling Rosewall in a match that stretched on and on. One sports reporter worried that he would not make his deadline if he waited until the end of the match to write his story. So he pulled out his portable typewriter and began typing. A few other reporters did the same. Soon the tap-tap-tapping of the typewriters annoyed Gonzalez. He shouted up at the reporters to quiet down. Assuming that Gonzalez was complaining about a situation on the court, the writers ignored him. Then suddenly, a tennis ball came flying through the press section.

According to one of the men,

> I was just working, not paying attention to [Gonzalez's] yelling until a ball parted my hair and crashed behind me. It was like a rocket attack, and we were, literally, sitting ducks in the front row upstairs. Pancho scared the hell out of us. I've ducked foul balls in the press box at Fenway Park, but they come one at a time, and the batter isn't aiming at you. Pancho was out to get us, hitting balls as fast and hard as he could. They were smashing all around us.[3]

Newspapers and magazines regularly reported on Gonzalez's outbursts. His talent for terrorizing locker rooms became well known. Writer Richard Evans told about the time Gonzalez was angry at courtside photographers because their flashbulbs kept distracting him. After his match, Gonzalez stormed into the locker room shouting and throwing rackets. One player hid behind a shower curtain during the tirade while another ducked under a table.[4]

Some people saw Gonzalez's manners as further evidence of his low social status. But many enjoyed his antics. Over time, he developed a large following of admirers. These people saw his passion for every point as evidence of a highly competitive spirit. There was a purity about Gonzalez. He did not seem to want popularity or acclaim. He simply wanted to play tennis.

Furthermore, Gonzalez's working-class background and Mexican-American heritage made him an underdog in the world of tennis. Many people respected the man's commitment to the sport and his solitary struggle to the top.

In addition, Gonzalez had a knack for charming the people who came to watch him play, even those who called him crude and obnoxious. There was something undeniably alluring about the handsome man who played ferocious tennis. As one writer put it, Gonzalez brought more "magnetism onto a tennis court than anyone who ever played the game."[5]

As for Gonzalez, he knew that his court etiquette was less than perfect. But he maintained that most of his poor manners were caused by frustration at himself for making mistakes. Furthermore, Gonzalez believed that showing one's emotions was natural and healthy. "For players under pressure," he said, "emotion is a way of stimulating yourself. In tennis, there is no [other] way to do it, and it's unfair to ask a player to hold it in."[6]

Gonzalez's opponents were not always sure he was simply giving himself a pep talk. Rosewall, for instance, said that Gonzalez's whole demeanor on the court exuded a "general air of violence."[7] Some people claimed that Gonzalez used his size and fireworks to intimidate opponents and referees. Rosewall himself admitted that he had to be careful not to let Gonzalez ruin his concentration. As Kramer put it, "Pancho gets 50 points on his serve and 50 points on terror."[8]

Those closest to Gonzalez knew that his explosive nature was caused by something besides trying to win tennis matches. They knew that some of his attitude was caused by an inner rage. Much of this rage came from Gonzalez's awareness that many people in the elite circle of championship tennis thought of him as inferior because he was different from them. This made Gonzalez feel awkward and out of place at the fancy parties and dinners the other players frequented. So he rarely attended them, preferring to stay home alone.

In fact, when Gonzalez was on a tennis tour, he spent most of his time alone. He ate by himself and spent his days in his hotel room, reading about cars. Sometimes he took a drive into the surrounding countryside. Gonzalez even traveled from stop to stop alone in his own sports car. Before long, Gonzalez had earned another nickname—"The Lone Wolf." And though he claimed to prefer his solitude, it sometimes had drawbacks. "When you lose you are down," he

Gonzalez was on Jack Kramer's pro tour for many years. Today, Kramer's truck can be seen at the International Tennis Hall of Fame.

said, "depressed and thousands of miles away from home which depresses you more, and tears come to your eyes. And you are all alone."[9] This loneliness may have added to Gonzalez's volatile temper.

Furthermore, Gonzalez was becoming more aware of racial prejudice. As his grandmother had predicted years earlier, Gonzalez did encounter blatant, ugly racism. One of the first incidents Gonzalez remembered happened one day when he and Segura were on tour together. They did not notice a sign hanging near a cafe door that said "No Mexicans served here," and they entered a Texas cafe to eat. When they sat down, no one in the restaurant waited on them. When Gonzalez learned why, he felt as if he would explode. But then he remembered his grandmother's advice and imagined the owner of the cafe in his underwear. His anger immediately vanished, but the pain would last a long time.[10]

When Gonzalez returned to Los Angeles after this tour, he talked with other Mexican Americans about racism. He learned that discrimination was an extremely negative force in many of their lives. Gonzalez was moved by their pain and resolved to do something to help all Mexican Americans.

Actually, his presence in professional tennis was doing more for them than he may have known. Richard Gonzalez was one of the few Hispanics many people in the United States had ever encountered, even if it was only through the sports pages of the newspaper. This visibility made them aware that many Hispanic people had been born and raised in the United States. These Hispanics were not Mexicans but United States citizens just like themselves.

Gonzalez's success also brought pride to other Hispanics. His determination to compete in a field that had previously been off-limits inspired them. Some

This sign is a replication of the kind often seen on businesses in the Southwest during the mid-1900s. It indicates that anyone of nonwhite ethnic heritage was not allowed inside.

took up tennis themselves. Others gained strength from his example and faced racism with more resolve.

In addition, Gonzalez served as an inspiration to working-class people from all ethnic backgrounds. He was an underdog—a lonely, solitary rebel. His life revolved around his love and his one goal—playing excellent tennis. Even those who did not like tennis could identify with Gonzalez's struggle in an unfriendly world. Most of them also struggled to achieve their dreams.

Sometimes it seemed to Gonzalez that this struggle would never end. Throughout his years on the pro tour, he and Jack Kramer were constantly feuding over Gonzalez's salary. Gonzalez often felt that Kramer was exploiting him. He believed he deserved a larger share of the tour's profits since no one could beat him consistently.[11]

When Kramer did not agree, Gonzalez made his complaints public. He told a reporter from *The New York Times* that he was considering breaking his contract with Kramer. Gonzalez went on to say, "I think I am entitled to the top position in pro tennis and that my record against Tony Trabert and Ken Rosewall and against other players in tournaments proves it."[12]

But Kramer refused to change the terms of their contract. This made Gonzalez legally tied to Kramer through 1960 or until he lost a tour title. This did not look like it would happen soon.

Gonzalez never stopped working to improve his game. As he had in his youth, he watched others to see what he could learn from them. Sometimes he copied a training method or figured out a new kind of shot. Furthermore, he practiced six hours a day on the court, then did off-court conditioning as well.

In the meantime, Kramer searched for someone who could beat Gonzalez, because he was tired of their fights. Kramer finally recruited Lew Hoad, an Australian he thought might unseat the champion. "If

Hoad could beat [Gonzalez] that was my chance to get rid of that tiger," Kramer reported. "[Gonzalez] knew what I was doing, too, and he was furious."[13]

Now Kramer did something he had never done before. Kramer took Hoad on a tour of Europe, Africa, India, and Southeast Asia to get him in shape for his tour against Gonzalez. In effect, he became Hoad's personal coach.

The Gonzalez–Hoad tour began in Australia in January 1958. It soon looked as if Hoad just might knock Gonzalez out of the No. 1 spot. The two played excellent tennis, and neither man was willing to yield an inch on the court. Many contests went to five sets, and some of these lasted for hours. As one observer noted,

> Both guys were such great players with big serves. Gonzalez would hit that serve, and Hoad would return it like a Ping-Pong ball. They would go corner to corner. Boom! *Boom!* BOOM! People would stand up and applaud, thinking the point was over, and it would keep going two or three more shots. Or two or three more exchanges. People would be screaming. I tell you, man, that was *tennis!*[14]

When the tour ended its Australian segment, Gonzalez was trailing Hoad by five matches. But then an old back injury began bothering Hoad and his tennis suffered. By the end of the tour, Gonzalez had caught up to Hoad and passed him by fifteen matches.

Gonzalez had won another pro tour. Curiously, though, Hoad had made $148,000 while Gonzalez went home with only $100,000.[15]

Gonzalez and Hoad also faced-off in the final of the 1958 United States Professional Championship Tournament. Gonzalez was victorious again. Now the winner of the most prestigious pro tour had also won the most important pro tournament in the nation—for the sixth time. Once more Gonzalez proved himself to be the master of tennis at its most grueling level.

In fact, Gonzalez seemed to thrive in the intense world of professional tennis. He even claimed to be having fun, saying:

> The hardest part of it is when you lay off and have to work to keep in condition. . . . While on tour I don't regard it as work. I can't go to the movies or watch television as often as I would like because of the eye strain. There are eight hours during the day when you have nothing to do, lying around for the match in the evening. It can get boring. But once I'm on the court I'm doing the thing I want to do, and I am very happy with my life.[16]

TRANSITIONS

 While Richard Gonzalez was establishing himself as the best tennis player in the world, his marriage was falling apart again. All of the traveling and training required of a top pro kept him on the road much of the time. When he was home, he was an avid pool and poker player and enjoyed bowling. He also liked to hunt and go to the track to watch drag races. Gonzalez's companions on these outings described him as charming and intelligent.

Henrietta was not impressed. Gonzalez was in perpetual motion, and she wanted him to spend more time with his family. Although Gonzalez said that he loved his wife, he knew he could not be the kind of husband she wanted.[1] So in December of 1958, the two were divorced.

In the meantime, Gonzalez worked with a writer named Cy Rice preparing his autobiography. The book was called *Man With a Racket* and it was published in 1959. Francisco Segura wrote the book's introduction, noting that Gonzalez was like a hurricane—with one exception. As Segura put it, "Weather is fairly predictable."[2]

In many ways, though, Gonzalez was entirely predictable. While on a tour, he focused solely on his tennis and preferred to be left alone. He stayed up late, drank beer and soda pop, and smoked cigarettes. Yet he still played excellent tennis. His powerful serve remained his biggest asset, and some people believed that this is what made him the world's No. 1 player. Gonzalez himself did not think his serve was any better than it had been during his amateur days. But, he said, his volley and ground strokes were definitely stronger. Most important, he noted, they were more consistent.

In 1959 Kramer again promoted a round-robin tour. This time Gonzalez would compete against Hoad and two other Australians—Mal Anderson and Ashley Cooper. Gonzalez won, then went on to beat Hoad in Cleveland for his seventh professional title.

On the basis of his record, Gonzalez tried to renegotiate his contract with Kramer once more. This time he gave Kramer an ultimatum. Until their differences were settled, Gonzalez refused to go out on tour. As he said, "Kramer needs me and I need Jack. He is the promoter and I am the star—the star who doesn't twinkle very bright financially. . . . Summing it up, the relationship is comparable to a marriage of convenience with mutual admiration entirely lacking."[3]

Gonzalez and Kramer ended up in court over the issue. The judge sided with Kramer, though, and Gonzalez headed out on the 1960 tour. This time he beat Alex Olmedo, Segura, and Rosewall. But for the first time in years, Gonzalez lost the United States professional title. In fact, he did not even make it to the final. That round was played by two men Gonzalez had formerly beaten quite soundly—Trabert and Olmedo. Olmedo took home the trophy.

By now Gonzalez had remarried. His new wife's name was Madelyn Darrow. Together they would have three daughters—Christina, Mariessa, and Andrea.

At about this time, a man named Arthur Ashe started college at the University of California at Los Angeles (UCLA) on a tennis scholarship. Ashe was an African American, and he had fought to gain acceptance in the whites-only world of tennis since childhood. UCLA had one of the most integrated sports programs in the country at the time. Yet Ashe

Gonzalez and his second wife, Madelyn, in 1965.

still faced discrimination there. For example, once he was the only member of UCLA's tennis squad not invited to a tournament at a private Los Angeles club. This snub left Ashe particularly angry. Fortunately, he had a friend in Los Angeles who understood what he was going through—Richard Gonzalez.

Ashe had seen Gonzalez play tennis many years earlier in his hometown of Richmond, Virginia. He had been impressed with Gonzalez's powerful game and even more impressed with Gonzalez's brown skin.

Seeing someone who had successfully broken through tennis's color barrier inspired Ashe.[4] So when he moved to Los Angeles to attend college, Ashe frequently visited the Los Angeles Tennis Club to watch Gonzalez practice.

In time the two became friends. Ashe worked out with Gonzalez regularly, and his game improved under Gonzalez's guidance. Ashe was grateful for Gonzalez's friendship, and he later wrote, "three stars shone brighter than all the others in my sky. One of them was Pancho Gonzalez, who was not only the best player in the world but also an outsider, like me, because he was Mexican American."[5]

Gonzalez won his eighth professional championship in Cleveland in 1961. He also won matches against more than a dozen players in another one of Kramer's tours. One expert explained that much of Gonzalez's success stemmed from his attitude. "Pancho seldom lets anything bother him for long," he said. "He'll go into the arena before a match and look at the lights—they're bad—and he'll look at the ceiling—there's smoke—and he'll test the court—it's slippery. So he'll shrug his shoulder, figure it's the same for everybody and then go out there and give it a battle."[6]

But now Gonzalez wanted a break from the battles. He was finally free of Jack Kramer's contract, and the professional tour was in a financial slump. So Gonzalez

Arthur Ashe, the first African-American man to win the United States National Championship, was grateful for the guidance and inspiration he received from Gonzalez.

retired from the touring circuit and moved to an island in the Bahamas that was being developed into a resort. Paradise Island would have a marina, a golf course, an elegant hotel, and, of course, tennis courts. Gonzalez was hired by the resort as its tennis pro.

Gonzalez's new job was to give lessons to various resort visitors. Many of the people who came to his lessons were nervous because of his large size and his larger reputation. But Gonzalez proved to be a patient teacher. Most people left having been charmed by his gentleness and sense of humor. As for the women, some were overwhelmed by his handsomeness. One even called him "a bronze Greek god."[7]

It was not long before Gonzalez was one of the most popular personalities at the resort. Guests enjoyed conversing with him whenever he appeared on the hotel's veranda, and Gonzalez was usually happy to oblige them. But he could be temperamental, too. On occasion he would cancel a lesson with little reason or apology. One island visitor claimed to notice a pattern in his behavior. According to this visitor, the more well-known or pompous a person, the more likely it was that Gonzalez would cancel that individual's lesson. On the other hand, Gonzalez was kindest to the ordinary, unassuming people who visited the resort.[8]

During Gonzalez's retirement from the professional tour, he coached the 1962 and 1963 Davis Cup teams.

He continued to be as devout a fan of this international competition as he had been in the 1940s. He even had a conversation with President John F. Kennedy about the Davis Cup in 1962.

The discussion occurred when Gonzalez was introduced to the president while he was touring the White House. President Kennedy was an avid sports fan, and he asked Gonzalez why recent Davis Cup competitions had been dominated by the Australians. He worried that United States talent was weakening. Gonzalez assured President Kennedy that the only problem with the nation's tennis talent was that it was young. Indeed, Australia won the competition in 1962, but the United States captured the Cup in 1963.

In addition to teaching and coaching, Gonzalez sometimes played a game called "Paradise tennis." Paradise tennis had been invented by the resort's owners. It was a mixture of tennis and Ping-Pong, and it was played on a huge table with a rubber ball and short tennis rackets. It was intended to be a novel game played for fun. But as usual, Gonzalez took the competition seriously.

In one tournament, he and Jack Kramer were doubles partners. When their opponents placed a shot close to the net, Gonzalez jumped for it, landing on the table on his back. His weight bent a table leg and the table sagged. Somehow, though, Kramer kept the ball in play long enough for Gonzalez to slide off the table and hold it up for Kramer. The two went on to win the match.[9]

While Gonzalez worked on Paradise Island, his wife Madelyn and their daughters stayed at the couple's permanent home in Malibu, California. Sometimes they flew to the island to visit Gonzalez. When the resort's tourist season ended, Gonzalez traveled back to California.

As usual, he kept as busy during these vacations as he did when he was working. Gonzalez often held tennis clinics at his California home, dreaming of finding a youngster to develop into a future champion. At the time, he pinned his hopes on his own fourteen-year-old son, Richard, Jr. Young Richard was talented and could even ace his father on occasion, something Gonzalez was proud to note.[10]

In the meantime, the professional tennis tour faltered. There was no tour in 1962 and Kramer's 1963 tour barely survived financially because so few people came to watch the contests. Some felt that this was because Gonzalez was not on the tour. Consequently, the promoters of the 1963 professional championship tournament believed that they needed Gonzalez if they were gong to draw a sizable crowd of paying spectators. To entice him to enter, they offered Gonzalez $5,000 in advance, even though the tournament's first prize was only $1,400. Gonzalez accepted the offer and became the only player to receive any money before the tournament began.[11]

When the other players learned of Gonzalez's unique arrangement, they were furious. Most refused to talk to him. "They won't even practice with me," Gonzalez reported, "but I'm going to win this tournament."[12]

Gonzalez's heart may have been in the game, but his body was not. The out-of-shape champ was matched against Olmedo who was in top condition. Gonzalez lost the first set, then somehow managed to win the second. By the third set, though, Gonzalez was so exhausted he could barely play. He later remembered how he felt near the end of the match. "My knees were so weak I couldn't stand up and my confidence and swing were also missing. If I hit an approach shot from the service line, I didn't know if it would hit the bottom of the net or the fence."[13] Gonzalez lost, and the tournament went on without him.

In the final round of play, Ken Rosewall beat an up-and-coming Australian named Rod Laver. But by then, the tournament had gone bankrupt, and there was no money to pay Rosewall his first place prize. The champion left with a handshake while Gonzalez, a first-round loser, walked off with $5,000.

Gonzalez had other worries, though. Mainly, he wondered if he could ever win at tennis again. He began training more seriously, and by the time the

Gonzalez returned to professional tennis competition in 1963, but he was out-of-shape. He rested whenever possible during matches.

1964 professional tournament rolled around, the thirty-six-year-old Gonzalez was well conditioned. This time he made it to the final where he played Rod Laver.

It had been raining all week in Boston, and it was still raining on the morning of the final. Even so, Gonzalez and Laver were determined to play. The two slipped and slid across the grass, but neither was willing to give up. It took Laver four challenging sets to conquer the old pro, and Gonzalez left the tournament feeling that he could still be a top competitor.

Gonzalez lost the professional tournament again in 1965. But in 1966 he competed in England's World Professional Championship and took home the first place trophy.

Now a new era was dawning in Gonzalez's professional career. Although he was no longer the best, he was still one of the best. Sometimes it was hard for him to accept that he was not going to win every match.[14] Yet there were still plenty of victories ahead.

THE NAME OF THE GAME IS STRATEGY

 In 1968 Gonzalez's twenty years in tennis were honored when he was inducted into the International Tennis Hall of Fame in Newport, Rhode Island. He was among prestigious company. Fifty-four others had already been inducted, including Bill Tilden, Ted Schroeder, and Bobby Riggs. As might seem the case, each of the other fifty-four players was white.

Gonzalez's photograph among the white stars of the game seemed a fitting metaphor for his unique place in tennis history. Even as he was being honored, he stood alone. Although Gonzalez felt like an outsider in tennis's elite social circle, he had drawn a large following of fans across the country.

People who had never played tennis before tried the sport after reading about Gonzalez's matches or seeing him compete. Many were from different ethnic groups; some came from working-class homes. Throughout the 1960s, tennis began trickling out of

In 1968, Gonzalez was inducted into the International Tennis Hall of Fame. Today, he is honored along with other champions in the Grand Slam Gallery.

private clubs and onto public courts. By the end of that decade, tennis enthusiasts came in all colors and from all economic backgrounds.

A vote by tennis officials in 1968 would add to the sport's increasing popularity. This vote made tennis tournaments open events, meaning that amateur and professional players could compete against each other. The United States Tennis Association (USTA) had considered open play for many years. Gonzalez himself had supported the idea since the late 1950s. But when he spoke of open play, Gonzalez always added one exception. He hoped that the Davis Cup competition would remain an amateur event. Gonzalez felt that this particular tournament should be played for national honor rather than for money.

As for the other tournaments, Gonzalez believed that open play would be healthy. Open tennis would allow more players to earn money. It would bring more competition to the sport which in turn would improve the standard of play among everyone. It would also increase interest in tennis. Gonzalez had been waiting a long time for open tennis, and he was anxious to be a part of the new era.

Others were not as eager. With more players competing against each other, some professionals feared their own earnings would decrease. Many also suspected that open tennis would be hazardous to their win–loss records. Their worries seemed logical.

For the previous decade, a relatively small number of professionals had been competing against each other. They all knew each other's playing style well. This meant that pros could develop their game strategies before a match based on their own strengths and their particular opponent's weaknesses. But open tennis would increase the number of players competing. Most amateurs were unknown by the current pros, and this made it difficult for them to develop pregame strategies. Gonzalez understood this danger, but he still looked forward to open play.

The first open tournament was held in Bournemouth, England, in April 1968. Though only a few of the best pros and amateurs entered, Gonzalez was there. In the second round he faced amateur Mark Cox, an Englishman and an underdog. Hundreds of English spectators had come to cheer for Cox. But as the match progressed, many discovered the irresistible lure of Richard Gonzalez and began cheering for him.

Unfortunately, the admiring crowd could not help Gonzalez win. Although he took all six games of the first set, he lost the second set. He won the third set by two games, then lost the fourth. During one short break in the action, he changed shoes that were waterlogged with sweat. It did not help. Gonzalez was tired while Cox was strong and confident.

Cox won the final set, making Richard Gonzalez the first professional player to be beaten by an amateur. After the historic event, reporters followed Gonzalez into the locker room for an interview. Most expected one of his trademark temper tantrums and waited guardedly for him to erupt. But Gonzalez was tired, not angry. "Somebody had to be the first to lose to an amateur. It might as well be me," he told them. "I was glad to be a part of this. Didn't think I'd ever see it happen. Now let me take a shower. I've been working pretty hard."[1]

Next came the French Open. Again many of the top professionals and amateurs stayed away, waiting to see the outcome of the new open tournaments. But again, Gonzalez entered. This time he made it to the quarterfinal round before being eliminated.

In 1968 Wimbledon was the first open tournament that included all of the best professionals and amateurs. Every player of consequence had entered. Ironically, in twenty years of tennis, this was only the second time Gonzalez had played in the tournament. The first time had been in 1949 and it had ended in a loss. On this second trip, Gonzalez lost again, saying he had played poorly because he was nervous.

Then Gonzalez began serious training for September's United States Open. There he played with such stubborn determination that he beat the No. 2 seed, Tony Roche, to advance to the quarterfinals. One observer noted that only someone who wanted to win terribly could work so hard for so long. And even though Gonzalez lost in the next round, *Newsweek* magazine reported that his performance had been the highlight of the tournament.[2]

In 1969 Gonzalez traveled back to Wimbledon for a third time. On this visit he won his preliminary matches and moved on to a contest that is still cited as one of the most dramatic matches in tennis history. In it, forty-one-year-old Gonzalez faced twenty-five-year-old Charlie Pasarell.

The first set began in the late afternoon. After more than two hours of play, the light was beginning to fade, and Gonzalez was having trouble seeing the ball. Three different times he asked the officials to postpone the match until the next day. Three times his request was denied. This infuriated Gonzalez. He cursed the darkness and ranted at the referee. He barely tried during the second set and lost, 6–1. Now play was suspended until the following day. As Gonzalez walked off the court, he threw his racket at the umpire's chair, and a group of fans booed his poor manners. This made him the first player to ever be booed off a Wimbledon court.

Back in his hotel room, Gonzalez fumed. He was too angry to sleep. He and Madelyn played backgammon until two in the morning. The next day Gonzalez walked onto the court refreshed and ready to play. Unfortunately, he had already lost the first two sets of the match.

But Gonzalez was not ready to concede. During the next two hours, the lead went back and forth as an astonished crowd watched Gonzalez fight back. A few people began encouraging him, and the number cheering him on grew with each point he won. Gonzalez took the third set, 16–14. Then he tied the match by winning the fourth set.

Now anticipation swept through the stadium, and all fifteen thousand fans seemed to be rooting for Gonzalez. They cheered each time he earned a point. They groaned whenever he lost one. Echoing the sounds of the spectators on the inside, another thirty-one thousand people tracked his progress on an electronic scoreboard outside the stadium.

Finally, it seemed that the great match was coming to an end. Pasarell was ahead in the fifth set, 5–4. The game score was Pasarell 40, Gonzalez 0. Then Gonzalez earned a point. Then another and another. Time after time, just when Gonzalez seemed doomed, he managed to stay alive. When the set finally ended in an amazing 11–9 victory by Gonzalez, the crowd exploded into cheers and applause.

As for Gonzalez, he was too tired to show much emotion. He and Pasarell walked to the net and embraced as spectators gave the men a reverberating ovation. They had both played magnificently in a record-setting five-hour, twelve-minute, 112-game match.

In the locker room Pasarell found a corner where he sat down and cried. Gonzalez took a seat next to him and patted him on the back. He told Pasarell he was sorry.[3] But Pasarell was not mad at Gonzalez. In fact, the remarkable comeback made Pasarell one more Gonzalez fan. He called Gonzalez's serve the best he had ever seen. He went on to say that Gonzalez "was a guy who would never give up. Somehow he would figure out how to win a match."[4]

In the next round of action Gonzalez lost to Arthur Ashe. Rod Laver would be the tournament winner. Laver's win that year was as historic as Gonzalez's victory over Pasarell. It was Laver's second win in a row at Wimbledon. But more important, Laver was on his way to becoming the first man ever to win a Grand Slam twice. A Grand Slam is when a person wins each of the four major national tournaments in one year. Laver had already done this in 1962. By winning Wimbledon in 1969, he completed three of the four tasks necessary for doing it again.

His possible accomplishment, however, was over-shadowed in many news reports by Gonzalez's victory over Pasarell. Hardly surprised, Laver commented, "That's Pancho for you, always stealing the show."[5]

Next Gonzalez went into training for the 1969 United States Open. He smoked less, watched his weight, and played tennis all day long. He also rested. This was a much more conscientious approach to conditioning than Gonzalez had practiced in his younger years. But Gonzalez knew that his age demanded better physical preparation.

One writer wrote that the most significant part of Gonzalez's training program was getting himself in a mood to fight. Gonzalez had retreated, the writer said, "to dwell on his resentments . . . and work himself into a mean, sullen mood, because that's the way he plays best."[6] Gonzalez responded by saying, "I've always fought, because I've always been pushed around."[7]

Although age was affecting some of Gonzalez's physical prowess, it was not dulling his determination. In fact, it seemed that Gonzalez fought harder now than ever before and that winning had become an obsession. Gonzalez explained his attitude differently. He said that open play had brought new competition to tennis, and he wanted to be a part of it.

Age had not detracted from Gonzalez's charisma, either. His jet black hair was graying, but he was still slim and fit. His magnetism and court presence remained powerful. As one writer reported, "Women find him fascinating when he steps on the court, gaunt and sinister, and begins stalking his prey. Men are intrigued by his hoodlum appeal, his angry and sullen manner."[8]

The organizers at the 1969 United States Open were fully aware of Gonzalez's crowd appeal. They expected each Gonzalez match to draw large numbers

Even in his forties, a well-conditioned Gonzalez could deliver a rocket-like serve.

of spectators, so they scheduled his bouts on center court where there was the most seating. In the meantime, higher-ranked players would compete on side courts.

Gonzalez easily beat his opponents during the first two rounds of play. In the third round he was trailing Torben Ulrich, two sets to one, when the players took a break. Gonzalez's feet hurt and his legs ached. For a few moments, he thought about retiring, saying he felt a hundred years old. Then he walked back onto the court and won the match.

Gonzalez was beaten in the tournament's next round. He was forty-one years old, and his age could not be denied in the physically grueling world of top tennis. His back became stiff and his nervous energy gave him stomachaches. In addition, his eyes seemed to be getting worse. Gonzalez wore glasses for reading and watching television, but he would not wear them for tennis. When he did, he had difficulty telling exactly where the ball was. Instead he took mineral tablets that he felt helped his vision. When a reporter asked him why he kept playing, Gonzalez replied, "Because I'm not smart, that is why. I like to punish myself."[9]

Indeed, Gonzalez was not about to quit playing because of his aches and pains. Instead, he found ways to overcome them. He practiced daily to keep his body in condition. He used an aluminum racket because it was lighter than wood and enabled him to gain fractions of seconds in speed. He cut the pockets out of his tennis shorts to get rid of the extra weight they created when they were wet with sweat. Gonzalez also stayed calmer on the court because he knew that anger burned up energy.

But perhaps Gonzalez's most powerful weapon was his mind. Hoping to wear down an opponent, Gonzalez looked for each opponent's weakness and played to it. He had always outsmarted opponents before, but now he honed strategy to an art form. Many players described Gonzalez as having the best tactical expertise of anyone in the game. As for Gonzalez, he said he would rather have the energy of a youngster than all of the knowledge in the world.

During 1969 Gonzalez was ranked as the tenth best tennis player. Yet at the Howard Hughes Open in Las Vegas he was able to conquer sixth-ranked John Newcombe and third-ranked Rosewall. He then went on to play No. 2 Arthur Ashe for the championship.

Gonzalez seemed to be on fire during this match, as he made one perfectly placed shot after another. Ashe even applauded Gonzalez after one outstanding stroke.[10] Gonzalez defeated Ashe and won the tournament.

Then Gonzalez announced his second retirement. During the past decade he and Madelyn had been divorced. Now the two were married again. Gonzalez wanted to spend more time with her and their children.

Part of Gonzalez's secret to success in his later years was game strategy. He spent many hours observing the players he would face and developing a game plan for beating them.

He also wanted to devote his energy to developing the tennis camp at his home in Malibu. But when the 1970 season opened at Madison Square Garden in New York City, Gonzalez was there. He worked his way to the final round where he would face the now two-time Grand Slam winner, Rod Laver.

Gonzalez knew strategy would play a major role in this match. Laver was not very tall, so Gonzalez decided to use this to his advantage. As often as he could, Gonzalez lobbed the ball over Laver's head and out of his reach. During the final two sets, his game plan began to pay off. After hitting Laver lob after lob that dropped just inches beyond his reach, Gonzalez surprised his opponent with a powerful drive across the net. Using this strategy, Gonzalez was able to beat Laver and earn the $10,000 winner's purse.

A week later Gonzalez picked up another $10,000 by beating Newcombe in a tournament in Detroit. A year later Gonzalez won the Pacific Southwest Tournament. Although Gonzalez was forty-three years old and supposedly in the twilight of his career, one writer observed, "somehow the sun never quite sets."[11] But even Richard Gonzalez could not keep the sun from setting.

THE OLD WOLF

 Richard Gonzalez's name dropped permanently from world tennis rankings in 1969. He had been a tough competitor for twenty years, but now younger men would take his place. As they did, tennis experienced an unprecedented growth in popularity.

One cause of this great boom was open tennis and the moneymaking possibilities it brought. More players than ever before were entering tournaments. This meant more tournaments were held. More tournaments brought increased exposure to the sport, which in turn, brought in more players. These newest tennis players needed to buy equipment and proper tennis clothing for their latest hobby. This made the advertising of tennis products profitable. Advertisements increased people's exposure to the sport and produced more tennis fans. Thus, open tennis created an increasing number of tennis enthusiasts.

During the 1970s city parks everywhere seemed to be overflowing with tennis players. New courts were built, and public recreation programs now included tennis lessons and tournaments. In addition, television began broadcasting tournaments. These broadcasts attracted large audiences that made advertising during the show profitable. Sponsoring a tournament brought even greater advertising opportunities, and the bigger the tournament, the bigger the benefit. Consequently, a few corporations created tournaments with enormous cash prizes.

Of course, only the very best players made it to the final round of these tournaments. But the ones who did were earning the largest prizes ever. Between 1950 and 1970, Richard Gonzalez had won close to one million dollars playing tennis. But in 1974 alone, four different male tennis players earned $200,000 each in winnings. By the end of the decade, the best players were earning close to one million dollars in one year.

Although Gonzalez did not share in the wealth open tennis brought, he was happy to have been a part of the explosion in tennis's popularity. He reported,

"I'm satisfied to know I was one of the pioneers, one of the guys who made the tennis boom possible."[1]

Gonzalez also remained proud of his heritage. Around 1970 he decided to make a public statement about his personal ethnic pride. He changed the spelling of his name from Gonzales to the traditional Spanish spelling with a z at the end.

In 1971 Gonzalez moved to Las Vegas and retired from the professional tournaments. There he took a job as the tennis pro at a famous casino called Caesar's Palace. By 1972 his second marriage to Madelyn Darrow had ended in a divorce. In December Gonzalez married a woman named Betty Steward. They would have a daughter named Gina.

Gonzalez suffered two personal losses during the early seventies. His daughter Mariessa died in 1972 after being thrown from a horse, and his father died of esophagus cancer in 1973.[2]

In 1973 Gonzalez was invited to join a tennis tour called the Grand Masters. The Grand Masters tour was designed for men over the age of forty-five who had once been the best tennis players in the world. Gonzalez had already competed against most of them, players such as Frank Sedgman, Alex Olmedo, and Mal Anderson.

The tour gave the old pros a chance to stay fit and play tennis with people of equal skills. The atmosphere among the men was friendly and nostalgic. They often gathered to play poker, socialize, and reminisce. Unlike the old days, Gonzalez joined these parties. He was often the first one there, in fact, and he enjoyed treating his old comrades to drinks. Many of these men noticed a marked change in Gonzalez since his pro days. Now, they said, he was much more easygoing and social. According to Laver, Gonzalez was mellowing.[3]

But the athletic Gonzalez remained alive and well. On the court his serves were amazingly fast, and he played in his characteristic catlike crouch. Yet curiously, Gonzalez did not win many matches. Some experts attributed this to his being out of shape. Others thought it was due to a lack of desire.

Gonzalez contended that he still worked hard for every point. He certainly demonstrated the same passion for winning that he had in his younger days. Amid the genteel atmosphere of the Grand Masters, Gonzalez was known to lose his temper and shout at an official or an opponent. Even nontournament games could be fierce competitions to Gonzalez. Once a bystander heard him challenge a friend to "suicide singles." When he asked Gonzalez what this meant, Gonzalez replied, "If he beats me, I'll cut my throat."[4]

By 1976 Gonzalez had assumed a new role, the role of the aging expert. Now people called him the "Old Wolf" and looked to him for advice about their

T ennis was a lifelong sport for Gonzalez, and he played until the final months of his life.

own tennis games. Gonzalez worked on another book called *Tennis Begins at Forty*.

In this book, Gonzalez gave tips for a different kind of tennis from the one he had played most of his life. The book described how adults new to the game or adults over the age of forty could play good tennis and have fun. Gonzalez himself claimed to enjoy the sport now more than in the days when he was constantly competing.

Gonzalez's mother died of natural causes in 1977. After attending her funeral in Los Angeles, he returned to Las Vegas and tennis. Now he was frequently asked to write for tennis magazines. Some of his articles gave advice, and others expressed his views on the sport. In one, he gave tips for longevity in tennis. "An athlete should learn how to rest more while he's competing," Gonzalez advised. "Players don't realize that the body needs rest. Invariably, they'll lie down after practice for 10 or 15 minutes and then wake up and find a couple of hours have gone by. Your body is talking to you. The same thing is true before and after a match. Proper rest is crucial to good preparation."[5]

Gonzalez was more careful with other health-related habits, too. In the early 1980s he quit smoking and developed a taste for the sport he had once described as dull—golf. According to Gonzalez, tennis and golf were a good combination for keeping his body in top shape. Keeping his personal life in top condition was more difficult. Gonzalez was now divorced from Betty Steward and married to a woman named Cheryl Duff.

At about this time, another change was taking place in tennis. It was led by men such as John McEnroe, Jimmy Connors, and Ilie Nastase. These new champions displayed court manners worse than anyone had ever seen before. McEnroe was dubbed "Superbrat,"

Connors was called vulgar, and Nastase racked up fine after fine for unsportsmanlike behavior.

Gonzalez was once asked to comment on the behavior of tennis's newest stars. "I think it's terrible," he said, "but I'm the wrong one to say so."[6] Yet Gonzalez felt there was a difference between his own court manners and the latest displays of etiquette. He explained, "I got angry myself, but it was to make me play better. If I cursed a line call, I did it quietly, for no one else to hear. This other stuff—the gestures, the four-letter words—it shows a lack of maturity. It reflects on the stupidity of the individual who, I guess, has no respect for his fellow man."[7]

Sometimes Gonzalez played tennis with his oldest son, Richard. They even entered father-son tournaments and managed to take home a few trophies. Gonzalez also kept active in Davis Cup happenings. This competition continued to be special to him since it was played for an entire country's honor, not just the honor of an individual. As Gonzalez put it, at the end of a winning match, the umpire does not say, "Game, Gonzalez." He says, "Game, United States."[8]

Gonzalez attended Davis Cup competitions when he could. In 1981 he watched his old friend, Arthur Ashe, captain a United States team. During a break, Gonzalez advised Ashe to be more involved in what was happening on the court.

Ashe protested, saying that he was involved. Sometimes, he told Gonzalez, he was so worried about the play that his heart was pounding. Gonzalez replied, "Well, we don't want your heart to thump too much, Arthur. But you have to *look* more involved, I guess."[9]

Being involved was something Gonzalez had done all of his life. Now he expressed unhappiness with the way Davis Cup play had become a moneymaking event. Gonzalez felt this was ruining its value.[10]

Another aspect of Davis Cup play bothered Gonzalez. In response to the disruptive on-court behavior of recent tennis players, the USLTA had written a code of conduct for team members. Any person who wanted to play on the team had to agree to follow their guidelines.

Some of the United States's best players did not like this new requirement. In fact, John McEnroe stated that he would not sign such a statement. Although Gonzalez did not like McEnroe's behavior on the court, he supported his decision, saying, "I wouldn't even give it a second thought. Under those terms, I would not play Davis Cup. I don't think anyone should dictate conditions on what I'm doing as a player."[11] Gonzalez saw the USLTA requirement as hypocritical and unrealistic. To him, the members were setting standards that they themselves could not live by.

Gonzalez supported young tennis players in other ways, too. For instance, he advised and encouraged one talented youngster from Las Vegas named Andre Agassi. Gonzalez met his next wife through this rising tennis star. Now divorced from Cheryl Duff, Gonzalez married Agassi's older sister, Rita, in 1984. It was his fifth marriage. In 1985, Gonzalez became the father of an eighth child, Skylar.

When Gonzalez's contract with Caesar's Palace expired in 1986, he did not renew it. Instead, he began conducting tennis clinics for conventions and corporations in the Bahamas, Hawaii, Palm Springs, and other resort locations. Rita and Skylar often traveled with him. For the first time in his life, Gonzalez was able to spend long periods with one of his children. He liked this new role and felt that he was more patient with Skylar than he had been with his other children. But as one of Gonzalez's brothers would later report, Gonzalez had a difficult time maintaining healthy family relationships. In 1989 he and Rita were divorced.

Of course Gonzalez continued to play tennis. Occasionally he appeared in a senior tournament, and as before, he always drew a large crowd. But now people did not come to see Gonzalez's brilliant shots or his relentless grit. These days people came to see the legendary player who had defeated so many tennis greats.

TENNIS'S BEST

 In the fall of 1994, Gonzalez learned that he had stomach cancer. The cancer began spreading in the spring of 1995, and by the summer it was out of control. Gonzalez was in so much pain he had to be hospitalized. Yet he was not about to miss the Wimbledon tournament that was just beginning. Gonzalez watched the matches on television, paying particular attention to Andre Agassi's games.

Lying in a hospital bed an ocean away from Wimbledon did not keep Gonzalez from the tennis court. He played each game in his mind as if he were there. Gonzalez once believed that Agassi was a better player than he had ever been. But now he began to change his mind. In addition to his trademark serve, Gonzalez knew he had once had remarkable speed and an outstanding variety of shots.

Now he began thinking that he may have beaten Agassi had they met when Gonzalez was in top condition. In fact, Gonzalez said, "The more I watch [today's players], the more I think they're not that great. They're good, but not as good as I was."[1]

Richard Gonzalez died on Monday, July 3, 1995. He was sixty-seven years old. Two hundred people attended his funeral. Many came to say good-bye to the man who had been their brother, father, or grandfather. Others came to honor a colleague and friend. Among these were Charlie Pasarell and Rod Laver. "You knew you were in for a battle every time you played him," Laver recalled. "He never let you off with any cheap points."[2]

Laver was not the only one who would remember Gonzalez's superb tennis skills. Many fans and experts believe that he would have won Wimbledon eight or nine times if it had been open to professionals before 1968. In fact, Gonzalez is often referred to as the greatest tennis player to have never won Wimbledon.

Like the fans of other sports, tennis lovers enjoy the challenge of comparing great players from various eras. For example, they might wonder who was a better player at his peak—Jack Kramer or John McEnroe. When the experts compile their lists of the best players from history, many place Richard Gonzalez at the top. Jimmy Connors once said that if he had to choose someone to play for his life, he would choose Gonzalez.[3]

Gonzalez's athletic skills were awesome and his knowledge of the game exact. But these attributes were only a part of his winning formula. Just as important was the man's competitive spirit: Richard Gonzalez hated to lose. As his brother once commented, "He wanted to play better than anyone else ever did."[4] He may have succeeded.

Yet Gonzalez's greatness went beyond the tennis court. He was the son of Mexican immigrants, a child from a working-class home, and the victim of hurtful discrimination. But he was also a brilliant success. This success was proof of what a man with determination and talent could accomplish.

Gonzalez never held himself up as a role model. He never joined causes or spoke out about racism. He simply became the best he could be. In so doing, he was an inspiration to people of all colors and a living symbol of hope for a better life.

CHRONOLOGY

1928—Richard Alonzo Gonzalez is born in Los Angeles, California, on May 9.

1940—Richard's mother gives him a tennis racket for Christmas. He soon becomes an avid tennis player who learns the sport by watching others play. In addition, a friend named Chuck Pate gives him tennis instructions and the nickname "Pancho."

1943—Richard plays in various tournaments to become the number one junior tennis player in southern California.

1945—Richard enlists in the U.S. Navy.

1947—After being discharged from the Navy, Gonzalez places second to Jack Kramer in the Southern California Men's Championship tennis tournament. He then plays in a series of tournaments, including the United States National Championship.

1948—Gonzalez is suspended from tennis tournaments for the first six months of the year. He marries Henrietta Pedrin, also of Los Angeles. The couple will have three sons. Gonzalez wins the United States National Championship.

1949—After winning the United States National Championship for a second time, Gonzalez turns professional.

1950—Gonzalez loses his first professional tour against Jack Kramer. As a result, he is not asked back on the tour for three years.

1953—Gonzalez wins the United States Professional Championship tournament.

1954— Gonzalez is invited back on the professional tennis tour. He beats three other top players during the year to win the tour. Gonzalez also wins the United States professional tournament again.

1955 -1959 Gonzalez wins each pro tour and United States Professional Championship tournament held during these years. He earns a reputation as a ferocious and short-tempered opponent on the court. In 1958 Gonzalez and Henrietta divorce.

1960—Gonzalez loses the professional tournament this year. He is, however, still victorious on the pro tour. Gonzalez is now married to Madelyn Darrow with whom he will have three daughters.

1961 -1963 After winning his eighth professional championship, Gonzalez retires from competitive tennis to teach lessons at a resort on a Caribbean island. During the off-season, he returns to his California home to conduct tennis clinics. He also coaches the 1962 and 1963 United States Davis Cup teams.

1963 -1965 Gonzalez returns to tennis but wins no major tournaments.

1966— Gonzalez wins England's World Professional Championship tournament.

1968—Gonzalez is inducted into the International Tennis Hall of Fame. He then becomes the first professional player to lose to an amateur in tennis's first open tournament.

1969—In a dramatic quarterfinal round at Wimbledon, Gonzalez beats Charlie Pasarell in a record-setting five-hour, twelve-minute, 112-game match. Later in the year Gonzalez wins the Howard Hughes Open in Las Vegas. Gonzalez and Darrow divorce for a second and final time.

1971—Gonzalez retires from tennis competition and moves to Las Vegas to become the teaching pro at Caesar's Palace.

1972—Gonzalez marries Betty Steward. They will have one daughter.

1973—Gonzalez is invited on the Grand Masters Tour, a new tour for the best professional players from years past. During the next two decades, the aging Gonzalez continues to play in other senior events. In addition, he writes about the sport in tennis magazines.

1983—By now Gonzalez is divorced from Betty Steward and has married and divorced a fourth wife.

1984—Gonzalez marries Andre Agassi's sister, Rita.

1985—Gonzalez's eighth and last child is born.

1986—After retiring from Caesar's Palace, Gonzalez conducts tennis clinics in various resort locations.

1989—Rita Agassi and Gonzalez are divorced. He continues to play tennis regularly and adds golf to his pastimes.

1994—Gonzalez is diagnosed with stomach cancer.

1995—Gonzalez is hospitalized when the cancer spreads. He dies on July 3.

CHAPTER NOTES

CHAPTER 1. THE BEST PLAYER EVER

1. Hal Higdon, *Champions of the Tennis Court* (Englewood Cliffs, N.J.: Prentice-Hall, Inc., 1971), p. 29.

2. "Purgatory for Pancho?" *Sports Illustrated*, July 7, 1995, p. 70.

3. Rita Agassi Gonzalez, "The Power and the Fury," *World Tennis*, September 1987, p. 26.

4. Thomas Bonk, "Pancho Gonzalez, One of Tennis' Greatest Stars, Dies," *Los Angeles Times*, July 5, 1995, p. A3.

5. Gonzalez, p. 26.

6. Cy Rice, *Man With a Racket: The Autobiography of Pancho Gonzales* (New York: A. S. Barnes and Company, 1959), p. 33.

7. Gonzalez, p. 27.

8. Ibid., p. 26.

CHAPTER 2. HE COULD OVERCOME ANYTHING

1. Rita Agassi Gonzalez, "The Power and the Fury," *World Tennis*, September 1987, p. 26.

2. Sharon D. Herzberger, *Violence Within the Family* (Madison, Wis.: Brown and Benchmark Publishers, 1996), p.109.

3. Gonzalez, p. 27.

4. *Current Biography Yearbook, 1949* (New York: H. W. Wilson, 1949), p. 230.

5. Gonzalez, p. 26.

6. Andrea Leand, "The Lone Wolf," *Tennis Week*, July 20, 1995, p. 12.

7. Elizabeth Bennett, "Pancho Gonzales," *Houston Post*, July 28, 1987.

8. Cy Rice, *Man With a Racket: The Autobiography of Pancho Gonzales* (New York: A. S. Barnes and Company, 1959), p. 134.

9. Peter Skerry, *Mexican Americans: The Ambivalent Minority* (New York: Macmillan, 1993), p. 23.

10. Paul Bauman, "Gonzalez's Talent Matched By Tenacity," *Las Vegas Review–Journal*, July 5, 1995, p. 3E.

11. Rice, p. 134.

12. Gonzalez, p. 77.

13. Ibid.

14. Leand, p. 12.

15. Gene Farmer, "Pancho Gonzales," *Life*, June 6, 1949, p. 71.

16. Ibid.

17. Leand, p. 12.

CHAPTER 3. CLIMBING

1. Andrea Leand, "The Lone Wolf," *Tennis Week*, July 20, 1995, p. 12.

2. Cy Rice, *Man With a Racket: The Autobiography of Pancho Gonzales* (New York: A. S. Barnes and Company, 1959), pp. 23–26.

3. "Mañana Comes," *Time*, May 19, 1947, p. 50.

4. Leand, p. 13.

5. Ibid.

6. *Current Biography Yearbook, 1949* (New York: H. W. Wilson, 1949), p. 231.

7. Rice, p. 61.

8. Arthur R. Ashe, Jr., *A Hard Road to Glory: A History of the African-American Athlete* (New York: Armistad Press, Inc., 1993), p. 145.

9. Gene Farmer, "Pancho Gonzales," *Life*, June 6, 1949, p. 72.

10. Ibid.

11. Rice, p. 72.

12. "Lazy, But Wonderful," *Newsweek*, August 2, 1948, p. 70.

13. Ibid.

CHAPTER 4. UNITED STATES CHAMPION

1. "Mañana Comes," *Time*, May 19, 1947, p. 50.
2. *Current Biography Yearbook, 1949* (New York: H. W. Wilson, 1949), p. 231.
3. "Indoors and Out," *Time*, April 4, 1949, p. 77.
4. "Pancho on Pancho," *World Tennis*, July 1981, p. 46.
5. John Sharnik, *Remembrance of Games Past* (New York: Macmillan Publishing Company, 1986), p. 255.
6. "Indoors and Out," p. 77.
7. Gene Farmer, "Pancho Gonzales," *Life*, June 6, 1949, p. 67.
8. Cy Rice, *Man With a Racket: The Autobiography of Pancho Gonzales* (New York: A. S. Barnes and Company, 1959), p. 81.
9. Ibid., p. 83.
10. Farmer, p. 68.
11. Ibid., p. 72.
12. Ibid.
13. Rice, p. 84.
14. Farmer, p. 67.
15. Allison Danzig, "Anyone for Tennis? Yes, Gonzalez," *New York Times Magazine*, May 1957, p. 42.
16. Ibid.

CHAPTER 5. PAST TENSE

1. Allison Danzig, "Champion Rallies to Score in 5 Sets," *The New York Times*, September 6, 1949, p. 33.
2. Himilce Novas, *The Hispanic 100* (New York: Carol Publishing Group, 1995), p. 232.
3. Andrea Leand, "The Lone Wolf," *Tennis Week*, July 20, 1995, p. 13.
4. Bud Collins, *My Life With the Pros* (New York: E. P. Dutton, 1989), p. 127.
5. Cy Rice, *Man With a Racket: The Autobiography of Pancho Gonzales* (New York: A. S. Barnes and Company, 1959), p. 157.
6. John Sharnik, *Remembrance of Games Past* (New York: Macmillan Publishing Company, 1986), p. 254.
7. Rice, p. 101.

8. Ibid., p. 107.
9. Ralph Gonzales, author interview, December 24, 1997.
10. "Pancho at 41," *Time*, February 16, 1970, p. 57.
11. Ibid.
12. Rice, p. 129.
13. Sharnik, p. 256.
14. Ibid., p. 255.

CHAPTER 6. "FIFTY POINTS ON TERROR"

1. "Best In the World," *Time*, February 11, 1957, p. 59.
2. Cy Rice, *Man With a Racket: The Autobiography of Pancho Gonzales* (New York: A. S. Barnes and Company, 1959), pp. 179–180.
3. Bud Collins, *My Life With the Pros* (New York: E. P. Dutton, 1989), p. 88.
4. Richard Evans, *Open Tennis* (London: Bloomsbury, 1988), p. 3.
5. "Pancho Turns Them On," *Newsweek*, September 16, 1968, p. 62.
6. Richard "Pancho" Gonzalez, "Freedom of Choice and the Davis Cup," *World Tennis*, August 1985, p. 80.
7. John Sharnik, *Remembrance of Games Past* (New York: Macmillan Publishing Company, 1986), pp. 255–256.
8. "Pancho at 41," *Time*, February 16, 1970, p. 57.
9. Andrea Leand, "The Lone Wolf," *Tennis Week*, July 20, 1995, pp. 13, 34.
10. Rice, pp. 134–135.
11. Allison Danzig, "Anyone for Tennis? Yes, Gonzalez," *New York Times Magazine*, May 1957, p. 42.
12. Ibid., p. 44.
13. Bud Collins and Zander Hollander, *Bud Collins' Modern Encyclopedia of Tennis* (New York: Doubleday and Company, 1980), pp. 107–108.
14. Sharnik, p. 257.
15. Collins and Hollander, p. 111.
16. Danzig, p. 14.

CHAPTER 7. TRANSITIONS

1. Cy Rice, *Man With a Racket: The Autobiography of Pancho Gonzales* (New York: A. S. Barnes and Company, 1959), p. 213.

2. Rice, p. 14.

3. "Pancho on Pancho," *World Tennis*, July 1981, p. 46.

4. Ted Weissburg, *Arthur Ashe* (New York: Chelsea House Publishers, 1991), p. 44.

5. Arthur Ashe and Arnold Rampersad, *Days of Grace* (New York: Alfred A. Knopf, 1993), p. 61.

6. Walter Bingham, "Champions in Trouble," *Sports Illustrated*, February 6, 1961, p. 8.

7. William Brinkley, "The Antic Arts—Pancho Gonzales," *Holiday*, July 1963, p. 86.

8. Ibid., p. 88.

9. Rex Lardner, "What's So Funny With Pancho?" *Sports Illustrated*, July 31, 1961, p. 27.

10. Brinkley, p. 93.

11. Walter Bingham, "A Legend Dies on the Court," *Sports Illustrated*, July 8, 1963, p. 19.

12. Ibid.

13. Pancho Gonzalez, "That Period of Adjustment," *World Tennis*, August 1987, p. 80.

14. Ibid.

CHAPTER 8. THE NAME OF THE GAME IS STRATEGY

1. Bud Collins, *My Life With the Pros* (New York: E. P. Dutton, 1989), p. 195.

2. "Pancho Turns Them On," *Newsweek*, September 16, 1968, p. 62.

3. Thomas Bonk, "Pancho Gonzalez, One of Tennis' Greatest Stars, Dies," *Los Angeles Times*, July 5, 1995, p. A3.

4. Paul Bauman, "Gonzalez's Talent Matched By Tenacity," *Las Vegas Review–Journal*, July 5, 1995, p. 3E.

5. Collins, p. 126.

6. Marshall Smith, "This Old Pro Is Just Too Mean to Quit," *Life*, September 12, 1969, p. 77.

7. Ibid., p. 79.

8. Ibid., p. 78.

9. Ibid., p. 79.

10. "Adios, Pancho," *Newsweek*, October 20, 1969, p. 105.

11. Kim Chapin, "El Pancho Grande," *Sports Illustrated*, July 7, 1969, p. 57.

CHAPTER 9. THE OLD WOLF

1. "Pancho on Pancho," *World Tennis*, July 1981, p. 46.

2. Ralph Gonzales, author interview, December 24, 1997.

3. Paul Bauman, "Gonzalez Mourned at Service," *Las Vegas Review–Journal*, July 9, 1995, p. 5A.

4. John Sharnik, *Remembrance of Games Past* (New York: Macmillan Publishing Company, 1986), pp. 259–260.

5. Pancho Gonzalez, "That Period of Adjustment," *World Tennis*, August 1987, p. 80.

6. Sharnik, p. 259.

7. "Pancho on Pancho," p. 46.

8. Alan Trengrove, *The Story of the Davis Cup* (London: Stanley Paul, 1985), p. 5.

9. Arthur Ashe and Arnold Rampersad, *Days of Grace* (New York: Alfred A. Knopf, 1993), p. 70.

10. Richard "Pancho" Gonzalez, "Freedom of Choice and the Davis Cup," *World Tennis*, August 1985, p. 80.

11. Ibid.

CHAPTER 10. TENNIS'S BEST

1. Paul Bauman, "Gonzalez's Talent Matched by Tenacity," *Las Vegas Review–Journal*, July 5, 1995, p. 3E.

2. Paul Bauman, "Gonzalez Mourned at Service," *Las Vegas Review–Journal*, July 9, 1995, p. 5A.

3. Andrea Leand, "The Lone Wolf," *Tennis Week*, July 20, 1995, p. 36.

4. Bauman, "Gonzalez's Talent Matched By Tenacity," p. 1E.

FURTHER READING

Biracree, Tom. *Althea Gibson*. New York: Chelsea House, 1988.

Blundell, Noel. *So You Want to Be a Tennis Pro?: A Practical & Mental Guide for Players, Parents & Coaches*. Cincinnati: Seven Hills Book Distributors, 1995.

Collins, Bud. *My Life With the Pros*. New York: E.P. Dutton, 1989.

Davidson, Sue. *Changing the Game: The Stories of Tennis Champions Alice Marble & Althea Gibson*. Seattle: Seal Press, 1997.

Edelson, Paula. *Superstars of Men's Tennis*. Broomall, Pa.: Chelsea House Publishers, 1997

Gonzales, Pancho and Dick Hawk. *Tennis*. New York: Fleet Publishing Company, 1962.

Harrington, Denis J. *Top 10 Women's Tennis Players*. Springfield, N.J.: Enslow Publishers, Inc., 1995.

Higdon, Hal. *Champions of the Tennis Court*. New Jersey: Prentice-Hall, 1971.

Rice, Cy. *Man With a Racket: The Autobiography of Pancho Gonzales*. New York: A.S. Barnes and Company, 1959.

Sharnik, John. *Remembrance of Games Past*. New York: Macmillan Publishing Company, 1986.

Singleton, Skip. *The Junior Tennis Handbook: A Complete Guide to Tennis for Juniors, Parents & Coaches*. Cincinnati: F & W Publications, Inc., 1991.

Wright, David K. *Arthur Ashe: Breaking the Color Barrier in Tennis*. Springfield, N.J.: Enslow Publishers, Inc., 1996.

INDEX

A
Agassi, Andre, 113, 114–115
Agassi, Rita, 113
amateur tennis (difference from
    professional tennis), 39–40
Ashe, Arthur, 81–93, 98, 102,
    111–112

C
Connors, Jimmy, 110–111, 116

D
Darrow, Madelyn, 81, 87, 96,
    102, 107
Davis Cup, 40, 42, 52, 85–86,
    93, 111–112
discrimination, 7–8,17–18, 20,
    22, 27, 37–38, 47, 49, 71,
    72, 73–75, 81–83, 116
Duff, Cheryl, 110, 113

E
Exposition Park, 23, 30, 32, 49

F
Flam, Herbert, 25, 26, 30, 32,
    33, 45
Forest Hills, New York, 5, 36, 43,
    45, 52, 53

G
Gonzales, Andrea, 81, 87
Gonzales, Bertha, 11
Gonzales, Carmen (mother),
    10–13, 17–18, 21, 22, 27,
    32, 51, 62, 110
Gonzales, Christina, 81, 87
Gonzales, Danny, 59
Gonzales, Manuel, Jr., 11, 14

Gonzales, Manuel, Sr. (father), 8,
    12, 13, 14–15, 17–18, 21,
    22, 23–24, 25, 30, 62, 107
Gonzales, Margaret, 11
Gonzales, Mariessa, 81, 87, 107
Gonzales, Michael, 59
Gonzales, Ophelia, 11
Gonzales, Ralph, 11
Gonzales, Richard Alonzo, Jr.,
    50, 62, 87, 111
Gonzales, Yolanda, 11
Gonzalez, Gina, 107
Gonzalez, Richard Alonzo
    (Pancho), Sr.
  birth, 10
  championships won, 7, 8, 21,
    25, 42, 45, 50, 54–55, 60,
    62, 65, 78, 80, 83, 90,
    102, 104, 111
  charisma, 47, 68, 71, 79, 85,
    99
  childhood, 11–17
  children, 49–50, 55, 59, 62,
    81, 87, 102, 107, 111, 113
  death, 114
  Grand Masters tour, 107–108
  grandparents, 8–9, 10, 22–23,
    73–74
  learning to play tennis, 18–21,
    23, 117
  marriages, 41, 59, 62, 79–80,
    81, 102, 107, 110, 113,
    117, 118, 119
  nicknames, 20, 47, 49, 52,
    55, 72

professional tour, 53, 55–57,
61–62, 64–65, 67–83, 85
reputation, 68, 72, 85, 96, 99,
102, 108, 111, 112
schooling, 17, 24, 26, 27–28,
29, 31, 46
teenage years, 17–34, 36–44
truancy from school, 24, 27,
46
U.S. Navy, 30, 31, 117
Gonzalez, Skylar, 113

H
Hoad, Lew, 76–78, 80

I
International Tennis Hall of
Fame, 91

J
Johnson, Oscar, 38, 60
Jones, Perry, 25–28, 30, 31, 33,
36, 40

K
Kennedy, John F., 86
Kramer, Jack, 30, 33, 36, 42, 53,
55–57, 60, 61, 64, 65, 67,
72, 76–77, 80, 81, 83,
86–87, 116

L
Las Vegas, Nevada, 102, 107,
110, 113
Laver, Rod, 98, 89, 98, 104,
108, 115
Los Angeles, California, 7, 9, 16,
17, 22, 23, 29, 30, 36, 41,
43, 59, 74, 83, 110
Los Angeles Tennis Club, 17, 20,
25, 32, 38

M
McEnroe, John, 110, 112, 116

O
Olympic Tennis Shop, 23, 29,
30, 49, 59–60
open tennis, 93–95, 105, 106

P
Pasarell, Charlie, 96–98, 115
Pate, Chuck, 20, 32, 47
Pedrin, Henrietta 40–41, 49, 55,
59, 62, 79–80
Poulain, Frank, 23, 29, 30, 32
professional tennis (difference
from amateur tennis), 39–40

R
Riggs, Bobby, 52–53, 55, 57, 60,
91
Rosewall, Ken, 65, 67, 69, 72,
76, 81, 88, 102

S
Schroeder, Ted, 5–7, 43, 49, 50,
51, 52, 53, 54, 91
Segura, Francisco, 57, 60, 74,
80, 81
Shields, Frank, 6, 34, 44
Southern California Amateur
Tennis Association, 26, 38
Steward, Betty, 107, 110

T
Trabert, Tony, 64–65, 76, 81

U
United States Lawn Tennis
Association (USLTA), 38,
40, 93, 112
United States National
Championship, 5–7, 8, 36,
42, 43, 44–46, 50, 52,
53–55, 84
United States Open, 95, 98, 99
United States Professional
Championship (World's
Professional Championship),
60, 61, 62, 65, 78, 80, 83,
87–89, 89, 90

W
Wimbledon, 50–51, 95, 96, 98,
114, 115